# The Garden Project

## Learning about sustainability and seeding healthy eating habits

### Within a STEAM framework!

By
Angelica Manca

Illustrations by
Ignazio Fulghesu

Hoopla Education

macmillan education

# > Contents

# > The Garden Project Walkthrough

*The Garden Project* combines the *Scientific Method* and *Project-Based Learning* within a pre-primary setting, supported by the following components:

## Teacher's Manual

*The Garden Project* Teacher's Manual is broadly composed of four main sections: **Introduction**, **Setting the Stage**, **Teacher's Notes for Units 1-4 & the End of Year Project**, and the **Appendix**.

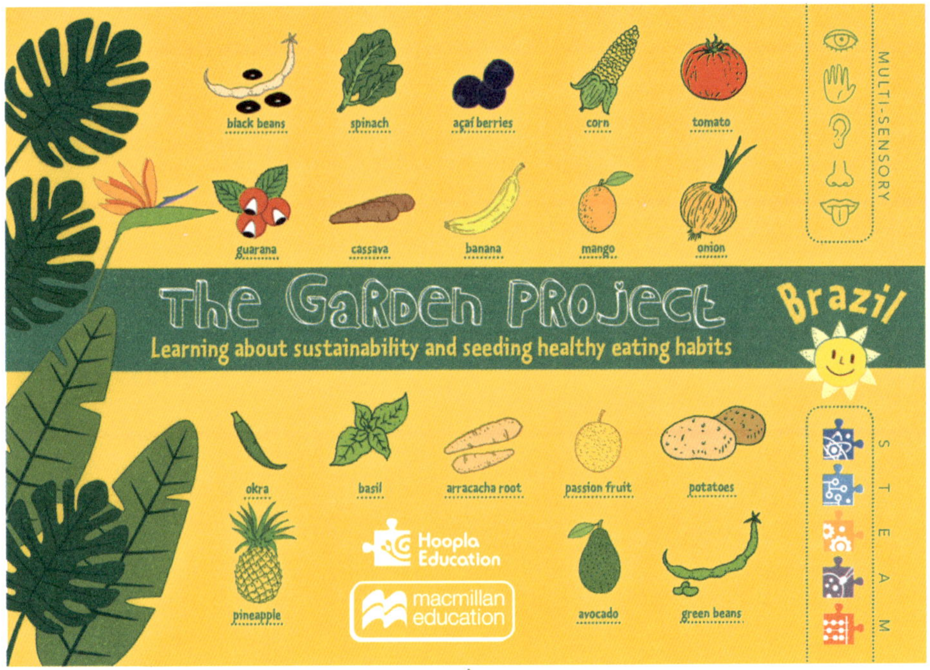


- The **Introduction** explains the philosophy and pedagogies that drive the project, strategies for the teacher to support student-led and project-based learning, and the student learning goals in each of the five STEAM disciplines. At the end of the Introduction is a comprehensive **Scope & Sequence** of the Project.
- The **Setting the Stage** section is a practical guide to preparing your classroom and gathering the required equipment and material for running the Project at your school.
- **Units 1-4 & the End of Year Project**: *The Garden Project* consists of four Units and an optional End of Year Project, each of which represents a different stage in the life cycle of plants. Each Unit is then subdivided into four Lessons with a defined and differentiated focus based on the student age. Each Lesson has the same basic structure, as shown on pages 5-7.

## Lesson Opening

The Lesson Opening page provides teachers with an easy-to-follow outline of the lesson's purpose and goal.

**Multi-Sensory Exploration** icons highlight the senses the students will use to explore and enhance their experiences in the lesson. See page 13 for more information.

The **Student Journals** contain skill-based activities that are subdivided into 3 levels – Wonder, Observation and Investigation – and document the student's learning process.

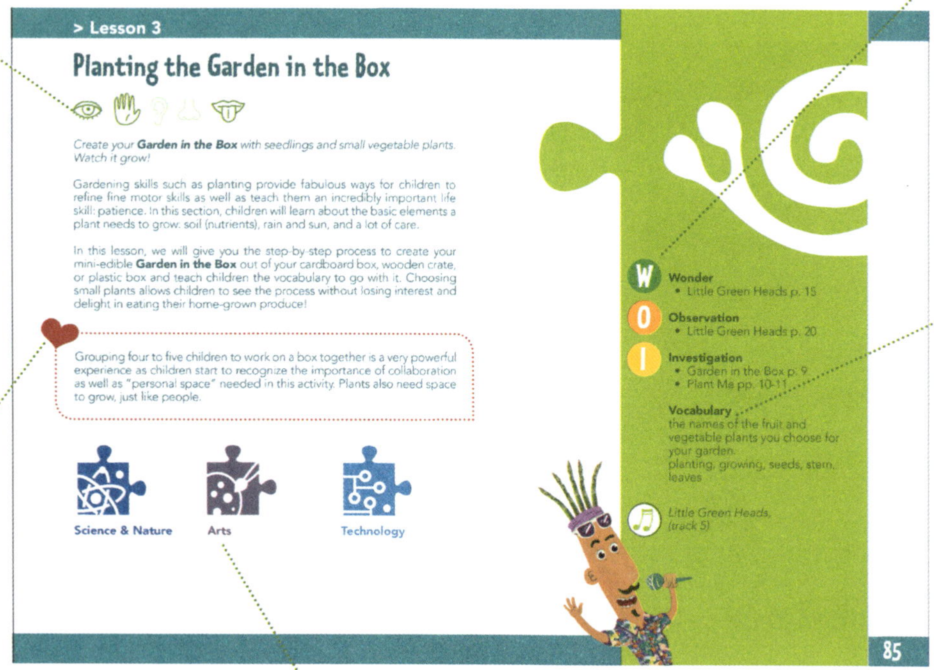

> Lesson 3

Planting the Garden in the Box

*Create your **Garden in the Box** with seedlings and small vegetable plants. Watch it grow!*

Gardening skills such as planting provide fabulous ways for children to refine fine motor skills as well as teach them an incredibly important life skill: patience. In this section, children will learn about the basic elements a plant needs to grow: soil (nutrients), rain and sun, and a lot of care.

In this lesson, we will give you the step-by-step process to create your mini-edible **Garden in the Box** out of your cardboard box, wooden crate, or plastic box and teach children the vocabulary to go with it. Choosing small plants allows children to see the process without losing interest and delight in eating their home-grown produce!

Grouping four to five children to work on a box together is a very powerful experience as children start to recognize the importance of collaboration as well as "personal space" needed in this activity. Plants also need space to grow, just like people.

Science & Nature
Arts
Technology

**Wonder**
- Little Green Heads p. 15

**Observation**
- Little Green Heads p. 20

**Investigation**
- Garden in the Box p. 9
- Plant Me pp. 10-11

**Vocabulary**
the names of the fruit and vegetable plants you choose for your garden.
planting, growing, seeds, stem, leaves

*Little Green Heads, (track 5)*

85

The **Vocabulary** list presents the new and recycled vocabulary that teachers can present naturally during the lesson.

Some lessons also have a **Social Emotional** focus that is elaborated in these boxes. See page 13 for more information.

The colorful **STEAM icons** indicate which STEAM disciplines the lesson focuses on.

## Lesson Overview

The Lesson Overview unpacks the content of each Lesson and provides an easy-to-follow 'road map' for the teacher and students.

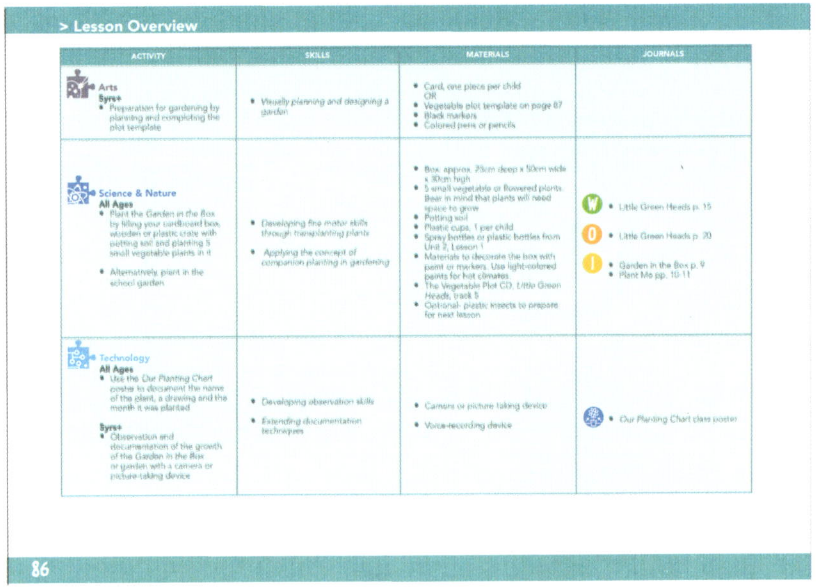


## Guiding Questions

The Guiding Questions frame the lesson inquiry and scaffold the learning.

**Our Green Question** is the heart of each Lesson. The ultimate objective of each Lesson is for the student to progress through the lesson activities and their own inquiry and arrive independently at their own answer to the Green Question.

The **Before and During the Lesson** questions provide relevant provocations and lines of inquiry to help student answer Our Green Question, while **the End of Lesson Reflection** questions ask students to review their learning and extend it beyond material covered in the project.

## Lesson Spread

Each lesson is made up of a series of activities divided into the relevant STEAM focus.

Activities marked with this icon require additional **Teacher Set-up** and planning time prior to the lesson.

A series of **Guiding Questions** have been elaborated to support children's understanding of Our Green Question and scaffold learning. These are the prelude to every activity, framing the learning in the activity and giving children clues to the answers pertaining to Our Green Question.

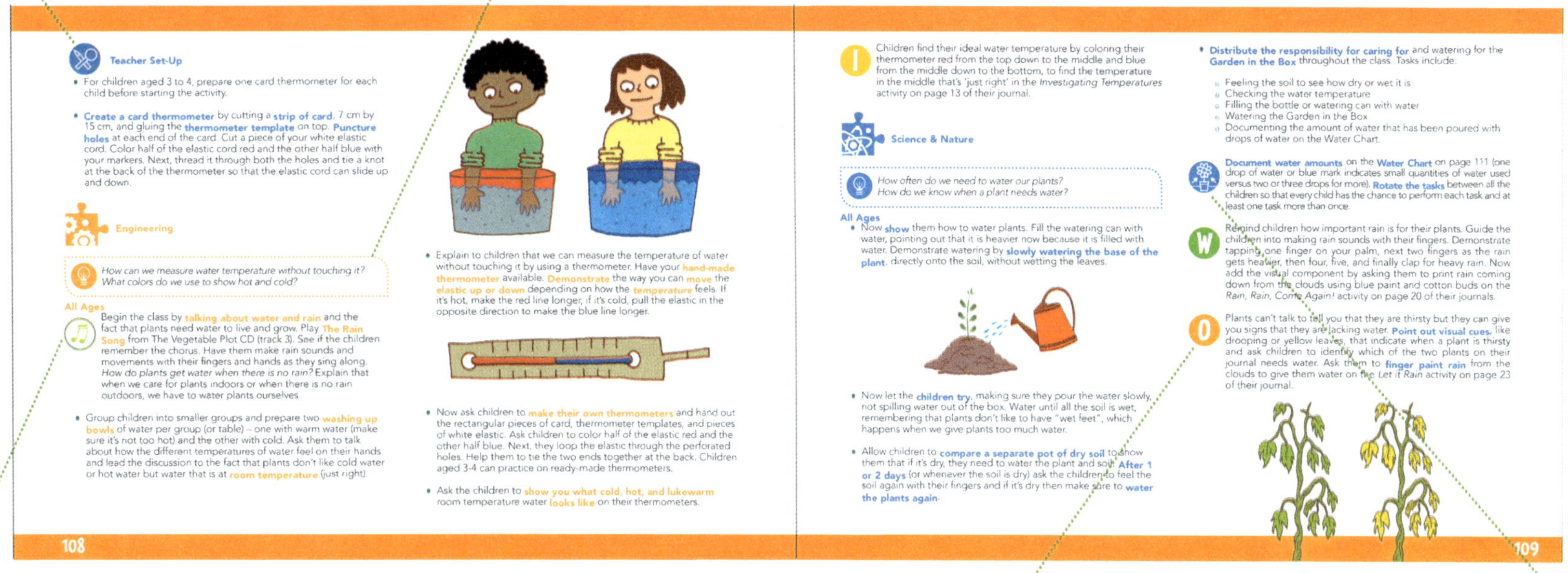

**Teacher Set-Up**

- For children aged 3 to 4, prepare one card thermometer for each child before starting the activity.
- Create a card thermometer by cutting a strip of card, 7 cm by 15 cm, and gluing the thermometer template on top. Puncture holes at each end of the card. Cut a piece of your white elastic cord. Color half of the elastic cord red and the other half blue with your markers. Next, thread it through both the holes and tie a knot at the back of the thermometer so that the elastic cord can slide up and down.

**Engineering**

*How can we measure water temperature without touching it?*
*What colors do we use to show hot and cold?*

**All Ages**

Begin the class by talking about water and rain and the fact that plants need water to live and grow. Play The Rain Song from The Vegetable Plot CD (track 3). See if the children remember the chorus. Have them make rain sounds and movements with their fingers and hands as they sing along. *How do plants get water when there is no rain?* Explain that when we care for plants indoors or when there is no rain outdoors, we have to water plants ourselves.

- Group children into smaller groups and prepare two washing up bowls of water per group (or table) – one with warm water (make sure it's not too hot) and the other with cold. Ask them to talk about how the different temperatures of water feel on their hands and lead the discussion to the fact that plants don't like cold water or hot water but water that is at room temperature (just right).
- Explain to children that we can measure the temperature of water without touching it by using a thermometer. Have your hand-made thermometer available. Demonstrate the way you can move the elastic up or down depending on how the temperature feels. If it's hot, make the red line longer, if it's cold, pull the elastic in the opposite direction to make the blue line longer.
- Now ask children to make their own thermometers and hand out the rectangular pieces of card, thermometer templates, and pieces of white elastic. Ask children to color half of the elastic red and the other half blue. Next, they loop the elastic through the perforated holes. Help them to tie the two ends together at the back. Children aged 3-4 can practice on ready-made thermometers.
- Ask the children to show you what cold, hot, and lukewarm room temperature water looks like on their thermometers.

108

Children find their ideal water temperature by coloring their thermometer red from the top down to the middle and blue from the middle down to the bottom, to find the temperature in the middle that's 'just right' in the *Investigating Temperatures* activity on page 13 of their journal.

**Science & Nature**

*How often do we need to water our plants?*
*How do we know when a plant needs water?*

**All Ages**

- Now show them how to water plants. Fill the watering can with water, pointing out that it is heavier now because it is filled with water. Demonstrate watering by slowly watering the base of the plant, directly onto the soil, without wetting the leaves.
- Now let the children try, making sure they pour the water slowly, not spilling water out of the box. Water until all the soil is wet, remembering that plants don't like to have "wet feet", which happens when we give plants too much water.
- Allow children to compare a separate pot of dry soil to show them that if it's dry, they need to water the plant and soil. After 1 or 2 days (or whenever the soil is dry) ask the children to feel the soil again with their fingers and if it's dry then make sure to water the plants again.
- Distribute the responsibility for caring for and watering for the Garden in the Box throughout the class. Tasks include:
  - Feeling the soil to see how dry or wet it is
  - Checking the water temperature
  - Filling the bottle or watering can with water
  - Watering the Garden in the Box
  - Documenting the amount of water that has been poured with drops of water on the Water Chart.

Document water amounts on the Water Chart on page 111 (one drop of water or blue mark indicates small quantities of water used versus two or three drops for more). Rotate the tasks between all the children so that every child has the chance to perform each task and at least one task more than once.

Remind children how important rain is for their plants. Guide the children into making rain sounds with their fingers. Demonstrate tapping one finger on your palm, next two fingers as the rain gets heavier, then four, five, and finally clap for heavy rain. Now add the visual component by asking them to print rain coming down from the clouds using blue paint and cotton buds on the *Rain, Rain, Come Again!* activity on page 20 of their journals.

Plants can't talk to tell you that they are thirsty but they can give you signs that they are lacking water. Point out visual cues, like drooping or yellow leaves, that indicate when a plant is thirsty and ask children to identify which of the two plants on their journal needs water. Ask them to finger paint rain from the clouds to give them water on the *Let it Rain* activity on page 23 of their journal.

109

Activities marked with this icon integrate **Music** and songs from **The Vegetable Plot CD** to get students up and moving and singing along.

Most activities conclude with the documentation of the children's learning journey in their journals, marked with the relevant icon:

- W Journal of Wonder
- O Journal of Observation
- I Journal of Investigation

Activities marked with this icon involve a **Teacher-led Demonstration** followed by **Group Documentation** on a chart or poster.

## Appendix

Finally, the Teacher's Manual **Appendix** contains the following reference material for teachers.

Copies of the **Skills Assessment Sheets** from the back of each Student Journal with age-appropriate assessment sheets for recording and reporting each student's progress;

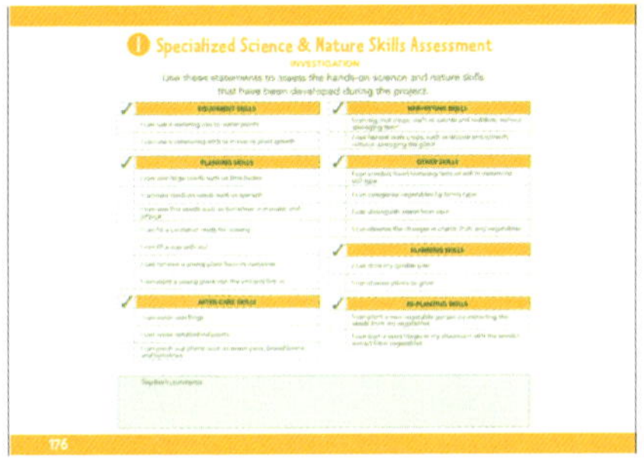


Categorized lists of **Vocabulary** that are presented during the project;

The complete **Lyrics** to the thirteen songs on The Vegetable Plot CD included in the project.

## Posters

Also included in *The Garden Project* are two double-sided multi-purpose classroom posters which help to scaffold students' learning and provide a place for the whole class to effectively record their observations and actions in relation to their Gardens.

## Student Journals

*The Garden Project* Student Journals are an integral part of the project and encourage students to document the world around them, building on their prior experiences by collecting, recording, and sharing observations of their learning journey.

The Journals are divided into three age-appropriate levels:

**Journal of Wonder (3yrs+)**
Students focus on nature's wonders whilst acquiring, recalling, and recognizing information related to nature's elements, parts of a plant, and how vegetables grow. This journal is an introduction to nature and encourages children to observe and question nature, and to get their hands dirty.

**Journal of Observation (4yrs+)**
Students are guided into observing nature's clues to have a better understanding of the world around them, as well as learning to care for living organisms. By this stage, students should start to recognize nature's cues and have a better understanding of their natural surroundings.

**Journal of Investigation (5yrs+)**
Students learn to use their observations to describe patterns in the natural world and record them to notice patterns over time. By this stage, children will have acquired a desire to understand and investigate nature and their surroundings and appreciate the importance of looking after the environment.

## Journal Activities

The Journals follow the same Unit and Lesson progression as the Teacher's Manual and contain activities that require students to apply and document their learnings from the lessons in various hands-on and creative ways.

**Learning Objectives** are provided at the bottom of each journal activity, together with the **Next Step** – an extension for fast-finishers.

## Student Assessment

At the back of each Student Journal is an age-appropriate assessment sheet for recording and reporting the student's progress. See page 12 for more information.

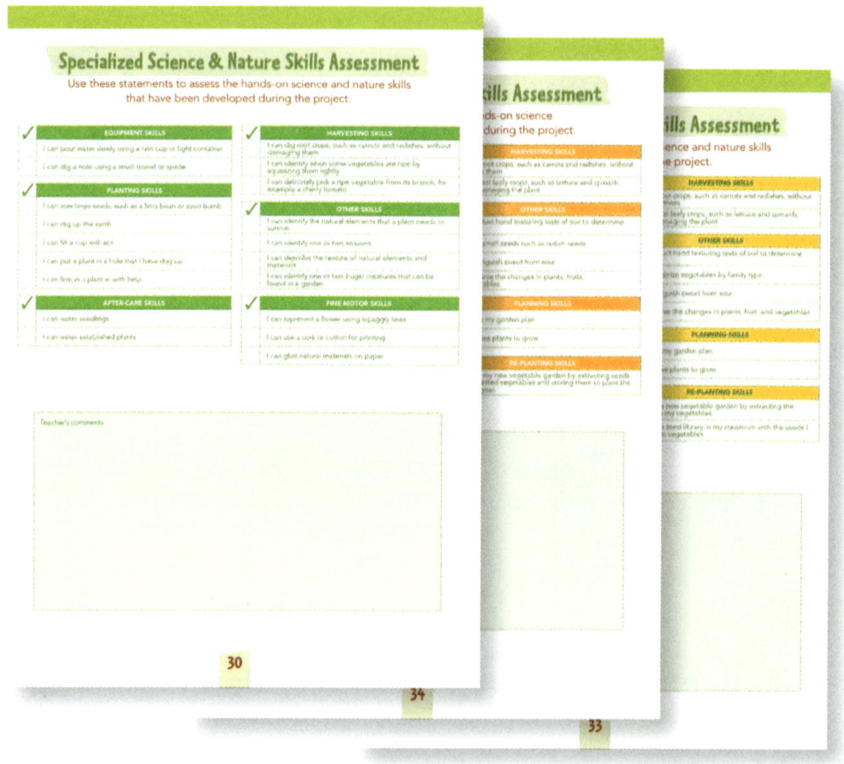

Complete the journey of these busy bugs in your garden.
Next step: I notice patterns in my everyday life

# > Teaching Strategies, Learning Tools, and Student Learning Goals

Specific to our curriculum are the teaching strategies and learning tools we have selected to help educators facilitate meaningful learning experiences for children.

Our teaching goal for *The Garden Project* is to instill in children a love of learning, to prepare them to view the world with eyes of wonder, and to grasp learning opportunities at any moment of the day! We aim to achieve this, in part, by helping children discover and cultivate their understanding of their ability to think, also referred to as ***metacognitive strategies*** and *critical thinking* skills. Metacognitive strategies facilitate children's ability to: (a) reflect on their learning behaviors, (b) identify their learning needs, (c) listen and communicate more effectively, and (d) adjust their learning habits accordingly. We facilitate this by providing an integrated curriculum that addresses the learning needs of today's multi-skilled, multi-tasking new generation.

## Teaching Strategies and Learning Tools

**Scaffolding**. *Scaffolding*, a term coined by Wood, Bruner, and Ross and influenced by Vygotsky's theory of "*zone of proximal development*" (ZPD). Scaffolding refers to the process by which adults or capable peers support and guide children's learning to a higher level of competence than they could normally achieve on their own. Scaffolding techniques are found throughout this teacher's guide and the learning progressions in the Student's Journal. Your role as an educator is to stimulate interest in the task by simplifying it, yet also providing the time and the intellectual support needed to keep the children interested in achieving their goals.

**Language Development Strategies**. In addition to providing a platform for learning, *The Garden Project* also gives educators strategies to extend vocabulary and introduce English as a second or foreign language in a natural context. Simple linguistic phrases are given to teachers to introduce new vocabulary following the natural approach, i.e. focus on "acquisition", the way children learn their first language or mother tongue, as opposed to language "processing".

**Music**. Music and Early Childhood Education go hand in hand, which is why *The Garden Project* has integrated ***The Vegetable Plot*** songs and music to spice up your learning journey. Children will be choreographing their own groovy dance moves to the music, in addition to learning new songs and rhymes that focus on planting, healthy eating, and expressing yourself creatively.

In addition to developing vocabulary, children are developing ***phonological awareness*** with the songs from The Vegetable Plot by focusing on the sound structure of spoken words while singing and rhyming their favorite tunes.

**The Vegetable Plot Characters**. In addition to taking children on a musical journey, we have adopted Aspara Gus or "*Gus*", the lead character of The Vegetable Plot, as *The Garden Project* mascot as he introduces key concepts and ties the learning together by giving suggestions and tips on healthy eating. Gus, an animated asparagus, is a fearless leader whose goal is to convey the message that vegetables love to be eaten so they can nourish our bodies. We hope that the emotional bond that the children develop with the character will also positively influence their healthy food choices.

**Specialized Science & Nature Skills Assessment**. At the end of every journal, the teacher is provided with an age-appropriate Specialized Science and Nature Skills Assessment sheet, to highlight the progress made throughout the project in those skills associated with Science and Nature. Teachers can either tick the skills that have been visibly mastered or mark the boxes with an "A" for *Achieved* or "IP" if still *In Progress*. It is possible to personalize the progress made by every individual child in the Comments.

**Social Emotional**. The social emotional component is one of the most important aspects of *The Garden Project* as, in addition to developing the social emotional skills between children, it also focuses on patience, caring for living organisms, collaboration, and empathy, which are key life skills we want to develop in all children. Students also deepen their understanding of the natural world as well as the environmental impact of their actions. Activities that have a strong social emotional component are marked with a heart icon, in the lesson introduction.

## Multi-Sensory Exploration

One of the strengths of *The Garden Project* is its highly sensory component. Children learn best when engaging their senses and can tangibly apply an acquired concept across a variety of settings. Every concept introduced in *The Garden Project* has a multi-sensory exploration across a number of disciplines, and they are highlighted in every lesson with the sensory icons indicated below.

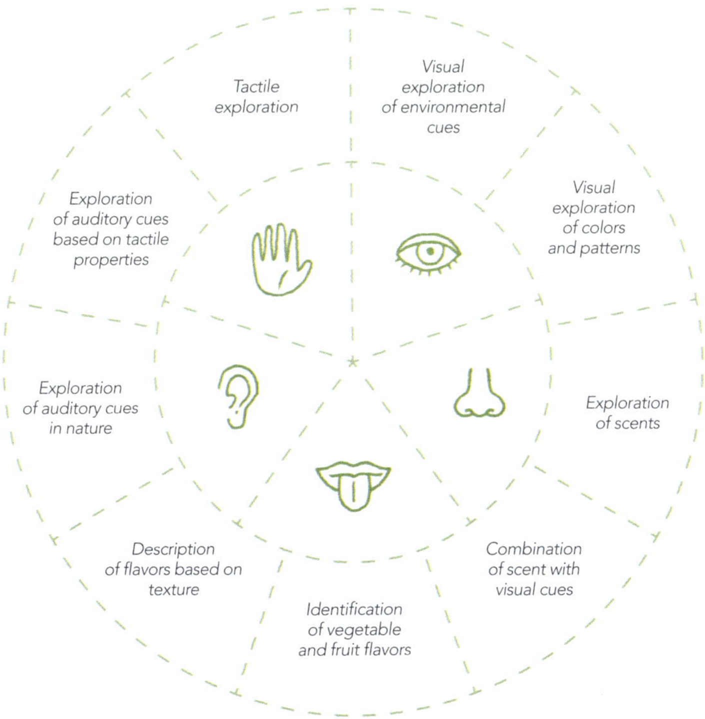

# > Introduction

*The Garden Project* is a standard-based curriculum that employs a Project Based Learning approach for teaching children from three upwards within a *STEAM* framework. The Garden Project values empowering children to build on their knowledge through inquiry of the natural world. Children gain knowledge and skills by working for an extended period of time to investigate, explore, and discover how fruit and vegetables are grown, using Science, Technology, Engineering, Arts, and Math as well as sustainable growing practices.

In the context of early childhood education, pedagogy is defined as the practice, art, science, or the craft of teaching. Pedagogy provides a shared frame of reference (a mutual learning encounter) between the educator, the young child, and his/her family. It is a dynamic, interactive, and collaborative process, underpinned by care, trust, love, reflection, mutual respect, and understanding.

The pedagogy guiding *The Garden Project* draws from several philosophies to create a dynamic approach to teaching and learning. These philosophies include:

**Project-Based Learning teaching method**
The Buck Institute defines **Project-Based Learning** as *"a dynamic classroom approach in which children gain knowledge and skills by working for an extended period of time to investigate and respond to a complex, question, problem or challenge"*. This allows the teacher to facilitate the exchange of ideas with the end goal for the children to understand, answer the guiding questions used throughout the lesson and exchange ideas on the lesson's concept.

Your role as an educator isn't to start the inquiry through a succession of questions from adult to child but rather a discussion, being prepared to speak, listen, respond, and put forward more than one point of view, with the intention of developing your children's knowledge.

Creating a discussion requires *you*, the educator, to take on various roles of expert, facilitator, participant, and creator of meaningful contexts for discussion and inquiry. Cognitively challenging and open-ended questions are most conducive to creative thinking and more elaborate investigations.

Below are the Essential Project Design elements that make up *The Garden Project (Buck Institute for Education, 2015)*:

- **Key Knowledge, Understanding, and Success Skills** - *The Garden Project* focuses on developing students' technical and metacognitive skills, which include critical thinking, collaboration, and self-management. In addition, *The Garden Project* promotes the development of intrinsic values such as empathy, respect, and patience.

- **Challenging Problems and Questions** – *The Garden Project* frames each lesson around **Our Green Question**, in which the lesson's objectives are focused on. Children are encouraged to respond to guiding questions in order to answer this and are thereby scaffolding their learning step by step.

- **Sustained Inquiry** – Children's innate love towards nurturing plants gives *The Garden Project* a framework for sustained inquiry as every stage of growing things gives children a sense of purpose and satisfaction. The duration of the projects varies depending on the age group of the children.

- **Authenticity** – *The Garden Project* uses natural materials and features living plants in a real-world context.

- **Student Voice & Choice** – Our child-centered approach gives children a voice and choice on the project, including how they work and what they create. Learning occurs naturally and authentically, as concepts are connected via the inquiry that is led by them.

- **Reflection** – Students and teachers reflect on learning, the effectiveness of their inquiry, and project activities. In addition, children rediscover handiness and the joy of coordinating the mind, body, and soul into action as they plant, grow, and care for their *Garden in the Box*.

**STEAM Framework**

*The Garden Project* applies a STEAM framework by developing child-led inquiry, as children are guided into discovering where their food comes from and how to grow vegetables *sustainably*. Age-appropriate skills – from categorization and, observation to problem-solving – are identified and woven together using Science, Technology, Engineering, Arts, and Math, as children's learning is highlighted through meaningful writing and journaling. Every activity highlights the adopted STEAM disciplines and how it interconnects with another discipline.

**The Reggio Emilia Approach**

*The Garden Project* is infused with the *Reggio Emilia Approach* as we too believe that the *environment* is a child's 'third educator' and recognize the many ways in which children interpret the world and represent their ideas and theories. We trust our children to ask the right questions and our role as educators is to intervene as little as possible, and observe, listen, interpret, and facilitate the children's research by providing interesting and stimulating experiences and resources.

## > The Garden Project Philosophy

*The Garden Project* sets itself the crucial goal of reconnecting children to nature with a 21st century framework of learning. Every activity draws its inspiration from nature to remind children and teachers that everything begins and ends with nature. Nothing is more inspiring than nature!

Educators are guided into using nature as an ever-changing set of resources that can easily be adapted for the local environment to employ instructional design combining all 5 STEAM disciplines in engaging lessons and mini projects in addition to developing critical thinking and problem solving through Project Based Learning.

Whilst gardening is a central theme of the project, it only comprises 20-30% of this science-based (biology and botany) project. Children are taught how to develop the scientific method, *the ability to hypothesize and set up an experiment*, as well as link each step of the growing process through documentation of their findings in their age-appropriate guided journals.

Math and Technology are used to deepen the learning experience as children learn to count leaves, make simple seed graphs as well as further their enquiries with the use of technology. The exploration and communication of findings is done through a highly aesthetic exploration of nature using, whenever possible, natural materials.

Finally, the social emotional component of *The Garden Project* is key. In an era where social emotional skills are at risk, it's important to develop life skills that encourage collaboration and harmonious living within our environment. In addition, children and teachers will have to trust the process as things will not always go as planned, but failures always carry important learning opportunities that are just as important, if not more, than successes.

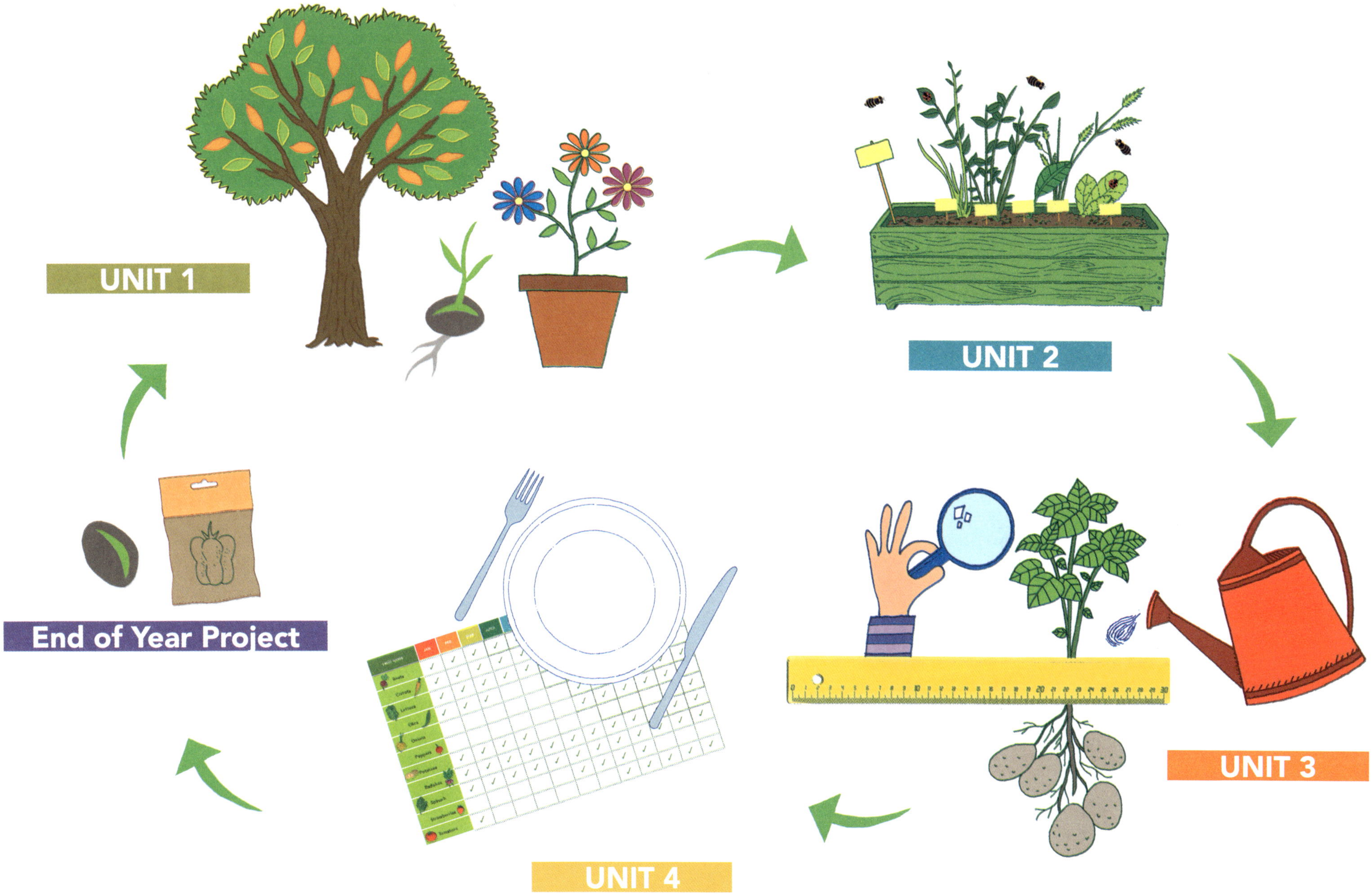
UNIT 1
UNIT 2
UNIT 3
UNIT 4
End of Year Project

## Student Learning Goals

Students experience integrated learning as they participate in lessons that are based on nature and also address development across key domains. Below are examples of the skills that are covered throughout the project:

### Science & Nature

- Adopting the **scientific method** by developing **observation** of nature and **asking simple questions** to gain a better understanding of their world. For example: "*What does a plant need to grow?*" or "*How do vegetables grow differently?*"

- Being able to form a **hypothesis** that drives **investigation** and **experimentation** is key to inquiry-led learning. Children are encouraged to carry out tests on the world to see if it will behave the way they think. "*Does a plant need water to grow?*" or "*Which vegetable grows faster – a radish or a carrot?*"

- **Documentation** of findings and **collection** of results is an essential skill for budding scientists. Documenting changes based on color, shape, size, height, and texture are some of the processes covered in *The Garden Project*.

- Throughout *The Garden Project*, there will be multiple opportunities for children to be **measuring** results, including time, temperature, and height.

- **Narrative skills** are a central part of the program as children learn to recall new vocabulary and describe the life cycle of plants, fruit, and vegetables in *The Garden Project*. **Vocabulary** is enriched through the elaboration of plant names, fruit, and vegetables.

- **Fine motor skills** are developed through gardening (sowing, planting, watering) and the use of tools such as magnifying glasses.

### Technology

- Children learn how to use technology **wisely** as part of **engaging** in **shared** learning experiences.

- The use of technology is encouraged as a means to document findings through **photography**.

- Observation and documentation are **deepened** through the use of **time-lapse** technology and voice recording devices to record findings.

### Engineering

- Fostering children's natural curiosity as to **why** and **how** things work in nature, especially when related to growing vegetables and fruit.

- **Devise**, **design** and **improve** solutions to measure and facilitate growth of vegetable plants, using **sustainable** materials.

- Learning to answer simple questions that arise in the process of growing vegetables. For example: "***How** do plants move their seeds from one place to another?*" or "***What** can we do to solve this problem?*"

- Following a **simple process** to find solutions which involves: **defining** the problem through words or images, doing the **research** to develop a possible solution, **designing** a solution, building a **prototype**, **testing** it and **evaluating** the solutions.

## Arts

- Using the arts as means of **expressing** an idea, feeling, and/or concept.
- Developing **aesthetic value** through **composition** of colors, shapes, patterns, and sounds is a key goal throughout the project.
- Children learn how to use a variety of **natural materials** (seeds, stones, sand, earth, water) and mediums (hands, feet, cotton buds, ink), to express themselves, such as with mud painting inspired by the *Land Art Movement.*
- **Trusting** the **creative process** and expressing it through exploration, experimentation, and intuition using specialized techniques (vegetable print-making, shadow stenciling).

## Math

- **One-to-one correspondence** in **counting** natural materials (beans, leaves, seeds) and developing early numeracy skills of division (splitting a vegetable in two), addition (adding seeds together), and subtraction.
- Children elaborate **shape recognition** through careful observation of the shapes of fruit and vegetables.
- **Pattern recognition** in nature, for example noticing that ladybugs have mirrored dots on either sides of their shell, finding spiral patterns in nature (explained by the Fibonacci series).
- As plants and vegetables grow, children learn to **sort** and classify/categorize vegetables in multiple ways as well as how to present findings using **simple graphs**.

*The Garden Project* is a standards-based program, aligned with key early learning frameworks. Below is an overview of the four units.

| LESSON | TITLE | ACTIVITIES | FOCUS BY AGE GROUP AND LEVEL | JOURNAL |
|---|---|---|---|---|
| **Unit 1 Preparing** | | | | |
| Lesson 1 | Season's Palette | • Identification of the seasons<br>• Identification of the colors by season<br>• Observations of local weather conditions | WONDER (3-5yr olds)<br>• Exploration of natural elements (from tactile to visual)<br>OBSERVATION (4-6yr olds)<br>• Observation of how plants can change the environment based on visual cues (seasonal colors)<br>INVESTIGATION (5-7yr olds)<br>• Use and sharing of qualitative observations of local weather conditions to describe patterns over time | W Wonder<br>• Season's Palette p. 6<br>• Today's Weather p. 7<br>O Observation<br>• Muddy Puddles p. 6<br>• Season's Palette p. 7<br>• Outside My Window p. 8<br>• What's the Weather Like? p. 9<br>I Investigation<br>• Budding Meteorologist p. 6 |
| Lesson 2 | Introduction to Plants and Plant Parts | • Definition of a plant<br>• Identification of parts that make up a plant<br>• Plant needs: water, air, and resources from the earth | WONDER (3-5yr olds)<br>• Tactile exploration of parts of a plant, combined with creative movement to support language development<br>OBSERVATION (4-6yr olds)<br>• Careful observation of the roots and visual exploration of a root system through a visual art activity<br>INVESTIGATION (5-7yr olds)<br>• Investigation of a plant's complex root system using a magnifying glass | W Wonder<br>• Leaves, Leaves, Everywhere p. 8<br>• Flower Garden p. 9<br>• Leaves and Seasons p. 10<br>• Forest of Leaves p. 11<br>O Observation<br>• Root Drawing p. 10<br>• Leaves, Leaves, Everywhere p. 11<br>• Patterns of Leaves pp. 12-13<br>I Investigation<br>• Root Drawing p. 7<br>• Leaf Insect p. 8 |
| Lesson 3 | A, B, Seeds | • Exploration of different textures (i.e. beans and seeds)<br>• Identification of the role seeds play<br>• Categorization of seeds | WONDER (3-5yr olds)<br>• Tactile exploration combined with pre-writing skills with the lentil finger drawings activity<br>OBSERVATION (4-6yr olds)<br>• Observation of the tactile differences between beans through the tactile bean memory game<br>• Documenting tactile differences in a simple graph<br>INVESTIGATION (5-7yr olds)<br>• Investigating tactile differences in beans | W Wonder<br>• Sunflower p. 12<br>• Bean Art p. 13<br>O Observation<br>• Spill the Beans pp. 14-15<br>• A, B, Seeds! pp. 16-17 |
| Lesson 4 | Reduce, Reuse, Recycle: Making Your Own Gardening Equipment | • Upcycling: making water devices from old plastic bottles and paper cups<br>• Investigation of the concept of recycling when upcycling is not possible | WONDER (3-5yr olds)<br>• Making watering tools from old plastic bottles and cups<br>OBSERVATION (4-6yr olds)<br>• Introducing the concept of upcycling<br>INVESTIGATION (5-7yr olds)<br>• Introduction to recycling and categorization of objects into recycling groups | |

| LESSON | TITLE | ACTIVITIES | FOCUS BY AGE GROUP AND LEVEL | JOURNAL |
|---|---|---|---|---|
| **Unit 2 Planting** | | | | |
| Lesson 1 | Let's Get Dirty! | • Tactile exploration of different types of "earth" (sandy, clay, dirt)<br>• Introduction to Land Art | WONDER (3-5yr olds)<br>• Discovering textures with 6 pots containing different types of dirt (2 of the same)<br>OBSERVATION (4-6yr olds)<br>• Observation of textures in visual artwork using abstract expressionism with mud<br>INVESTIGATION (5-7yr olds)<br>• Investigating the effects of water on mud texture and visually displaying findings through abstract expressionism with mud | W Wonder<br>• Muddy Print p. 14<br>O Observation<br>• Mud Drawing p. 18 |
| Lesson 2 | Companion Planting | • Introduction and exploration of the concept of cooperation and collaboration through plants<br>• Plant combinations | WONDER (3-5yr olds)<br>• Combining plants together to introduce the concept of working together<br>OBSERVATION (4-6yr olds)<br>• Further developing the concepts of plant combinations with fine motor skills<br>INVESTIGATION (5-7yr olds)<br>• Application of the concept of cooperation in the classroom | O Observation<br>• My Companion Plants p. 19 |
| Lesson 3 | Planting the Garden in the Box | • Plant, transplant, and seedling placement of the Garden in the Box<br>• Labelling of plants<br>• Development of planning skills related to gardening and identifying patterns over time | WONDER (3-5yr olds)<br>• Playing with dirt and planting<br>OBSERVATION (4-6yr olds)<br>• Planting and planning where to position plants<br>INVESTIGATION (5-7yr olds)<br>• Planning the Garden in the Box and combining with companion planting | W Wonder<br>• Little Green Heads p. 15<br>O Observation<br>• Little Green Heads p. 20<br>I Investigation<br>• Garden in the Box p. 9<br>• Plant Me pp. 10-11 |
| Lesson 4 | Friends of the Garden | • Categorization of certain creatures as being friends or pests of the garden<br>• Identification of bees as pollinators<br>• Conceptualizing the role of pollinators in the growth of certain vegetables | WONDER (3-5yr olds)<br>• Identifying a simple pattern. Understanding the difference between a friend and a pest in the garden<br>OBSERVATION (4-6yr olds)<br>• Observation of a simple pattern in a drawing inspired by Aboriginal Australian storytelling<br>INVESTIGATION (5-7yr olds)<br>• Pattern completion in a drawing inspired by Aboriginal Australian storytelling<br>• Developing early numeracy through the ladybugs counting game | W Wonder<br>• Friends or Pests? Friends! p. 16<br>• Friends or Pests? Pests! p.17<br>• Friends of the Garden pp. 18-19<br>O Observation<br>• Busy Bees p. 21<br>• Friends of the Garden p. 22<br>I Investigation<br>• Ladybug Spots p. 12 |

| LESSON | TITLE | ACTIVITIES | FOCUS BY AGE GROUP AND LEVEL | JOURNAL |
|---|---|---|---|---|
| **Unit 3 Growing** | | | | |
| Lesson 1 | Caring for Plants: Watering and Water's Properties | • Sound exploration of water or rain<br>• Caring for plants through watering<br>• Development of gardening skills such as transplanting and thinning out | WONDER (3-5yr olds)<br>• Sound exploration of water and the watering of plants<br>OBSERVATION (4-6yr olds)<br>• Observing plant needs and documenting their watering patterns<br>INVESTIGATION (5-7yr olds)<br>• Investigating optimal water temperature for plants<br>• Perfecting fine motor skills through thinning out | W Wonder<br>• Rain, Rain, Come Again! p. 20<br>O Observation<br>• Let It Rain! p. 23<br>I Investigation<br>• Investigating Temperature p. 13 |
| Lesson 2 | Observing and Documenting a Life Cycle | • Revision of seeds and their role<br>• Observation of a seed's life cycle from 1 to 20 days<br>• Documentation of a seed's life cycle, from 1 to 20 days | WONDER (3-5yr olds)<br>• Planting a seed<br>OBSERVATION (4-6yr olds)<br>• Planting a seed and observing the different stages of a sprout<br>INVESTIGATION (5-7yr olds)<br>• Planting a seed, observing and documenting the different stages of a sprout | W Wonder<br>• Sprouting a Seed p. 21<br>O Observation<br>• Observing a Life Cycle p. 24<br>I Investigation<br>• Life Cycle Journal pp. 14-15 |
| Lesson 3 | Discovering Fruit & Vegetable Shapes | • Introduction to shapes<br>• Exploration of vegetable shapes through a visual activity (vegetable printing)<br>• Exploration of sweet and sour and connecting tastes to fresh fruit | WONDER (3-5yr olds)<br>• Exploring vegetables shapes by creating a landscape using a vegetable printing technique<br>OBSERVATION (4-6yr olds)<br>• Identifying shapes in nature and transforming shapes into fruits and vegetables<br>INVESTIGATION (5-7yr olds)<br>• Investigating shapes and applying early numeracy to nature by counting the layers of an onion | W Wonder<br>• Foodscape pp. 22-23<br>O Observation<br>• Triangles and Circles and Squares... Oh My! p. 25<br>I Investigation<br>• X-Ray Onions p. 16 |
| Lesson 4 | Watch the Plants Grow | • Development of the concept of measurement<br>• Development of observation skills through measurement<br>• Recording of data through documentation of plant growth | WONDER (3-5yr olds)<br>• Supporting language development and enhancing the concept of "growing" through creative movement<br>OBSERVATION (4-6yr olds)<br>• Introducing the basic concept of measurement as an instrument to observe change<br>INVESTIGATION (5-7yr olds)<br>• Investigating plant growth through measurement and documentation | O Observation<br>• Observing Fruits in Nature p. 26<br>I Investigation<br>• See How They Grow p. 17<br>• Measure Me! pp. 18-19<br>• Plant Growth Chart pp. 20-21 |

| LESSON | TITLE | ACTIVITIES | FOCUS BY AGE GROUP AND LEVEL | JOURNAL |
|---|---|---|---|---|
| | | | **Unit 4 Harvesting** | |
| Lesson 1 | Vegetable Families | • Development of early numeracy by counting vegetables<br>• Classification of vegetables (family groups)<br>• Exploration of high and low pitches through vegetable instruments | WONDER (3-5yr olds)<br>• Identifying differences and similarities in vegetables<br>OBSERVATION (4-6yr olds)<br>• Categorizing vegetables by type and color<br>INVESTIGATION (5-7yr olds)<br>• Categorizing vegetables by family types and connecting this concept with the child's family tree. Applying their sense of creativity to use vegetables to create simple instruments | I Investigation<br>• Vegetable Families pp. 22-23<br>• My Family Tree p. 24 |
| Lesson 2 | How Did Your Vegetables Grow? | • Use of basic mathematical language to describe concepts of position and size (comparison)<br>• Identification of vegetable maturity, i.e. when they are ready to be picked | WONDER (3-5yr olds)<br>• Learning to identify which vegetables grow above and below the ground<br>OBSERVATION (4-6yr olds)<br>• Describing how vegetables grow and noticing when they are ready to be picked or harvested<br>INVESTIGATION (5-7yr olds)<br>• Investigating the shapes of ripe fruits and vegetables in nature through mandalas and thaumatropes | W Wonder<br>• Carrots and Cassava p. 24<br>• Squeeze Your Vegetables p. 25<br>O Observation<br>• Developing My Sense of Taste p. 27<br>I Investigation<br>• Above and Under the Ground p.25 |
| Lesson 3 | Eating by Season | • Identification of fruit and vegetable seasonality<br>• Documentation of seasonality through a harvest chart | WONDER (3-5yr olds)<br>• Understanding the seasonality of fruit and vegetables<br>OBSERVATION (4-6yr olds)<br>• Connecting the seasonality of fruits and vegetables with the color wheel<br>INVESTIGATION (5-7yr olds)<br>• Documenting and charting the seasonality of the vegetables that have been grown throughout The Garden Project | W Wonder<br>• At the Market p. 26<br>O Observation<br>• Fruit and Vegetables Color Wheel p. 28<br>I Investigation<br>• My Harvest Chart p. 26-27 |
| Lesson 4 | Eating the Rainbow | • Revision of colors<br>• Introduction to nutrition and healthy eating by color<br>• Categorization of vegetables by color groups | WONDER (3-5yr olds)<br>• Identifying that vegetables have bright colors<br>OBSERVATION (4-6yr olds)<br>• Identifying vegetables by color groups<br>INVESTIGATION (5-7yr olds)<br>• Categorizing vegetables by color groups and making simple healthy choices for a snack | W Wonder<br>• Colorful Vegetables p. 27<br>O Observation<br>• Eating the Rainbow! p 29<br>• My Favorite Recipe p. 30<br>• What's for Dinner? p. 31<br>I Investigation<br>• Creative Juices p. 28<br>• Fruit Mandalas p. 29<br>• Fruit Thaumatrope p. 30 |

| TITLE | ACTIVITIES | FOCUS BY GROUP AND LEVEL |
|---|---|---|
| **Seed You Next Year** | | |
| Seed You Next Year | • Seeds and the promise for new life<br>• Extracting seeds<br>• Planning next year's Garden in the Box<br>• Making seed bombs | WONDER (3-5yr olds)<br>• Extracting seeds and revising their role in a plant life cycle<br>OBSERVATION (4-6yr olds)<br>• Noticing the role seeds play in continuing the life cycle and extracting seeds<br>INVESTIGATION (5-7yr olds)<br>• Developing a more elaborate sense of timing through the life cycle of a plant. Creating seed packets to prepare the following year's Garden in the Box |

# > SETTING THE STAGE

In this section, you will find a list of practical resources that will help you plan and make the most of *The Garden Project* at your school. We will guide you through a number of aspects you will have to consider as you start organizing your garden space, timing, and program.

- Space
- Safety and Allergies
- Timing of Activities
- Seeds vs. Seedlings
- Specialized Garden Equipment
- Specialized Technology Equipment
- Time Frame
- Planning
- Expectations

## Seasonality

*The Garden Project* will vary greatly according to the month or season you are running the project in. Select a minimum of 5 to a maximum of 10 different vegetable plants you will use. Keep it simple by choosing one plant per color group and/or vegetable type.
Please be aware that the seasonality of fruit and vegetables is highly dependent on the climate of your region. The example planting table on page 81 and the harvest chart on page 150 reflect a tropical climate with wet and dry seasons, which may not necessarily reflect your local climate. It is best to check seasonality at your local plant nursery or garden shop when getting plants and seeds to ensure your chosen plants will thrive.

Complete the chart below with the vegetables you plan to plant by month, categorized into six color groups:

| | | | |
|---|---|---|---|
| **January** | | | |
| **February** | | | |
| **March** | | | |
| **April** | | | |
| **May** | | | |
| **June** | | | |
| **July** | | | |
| **August** | | | |
| **September** | | | |
| **October** | | | |
| **November** | | | |
| **December** | | | |

| | | | |
|---|---|---|---|
| | | | January |
| | | | February |
| | | | March |
| | | | April |
| | | | May |
| | | | June |
| | | | July |
| | | | August |
| | | | September |
| | | | October |
| | | | November |
| | | | December |

## Space

Before you start planting, it is a good idea to spend time planning how and where you hope to grow in whatever space is available to you. The beauty of *The Garden Project* is that it can be done both inside or outside thanks to practical portable boxes that can be moved around as needed.

Even if you have an outdoor space, we encourage each classroom to grow their own Garden in the Box. The advantage is that children are able to observe the daily growth of their fruit and vegetables, a rich and invaluable experience for your students.

However, keep in mind that vegetable plants will need time outdoors to get pollinated to bear fruit. In addition, whether indoors or outside, you will have to place the boxes in a sunny place where plants can get a minimum of 4 hours of direct sunlight.

See an example of a Garden in the Box below:

Now it's your turn! Complete the chart with the fruit and vegetable plants you will plant:

If you've decided to create an outdoor garden, consider marking the sections off with a special boundary, gate or decorative entrance.
If you have the advantage of having an outdoor area or garden in which you can plant in at school, you have more space to grow a variety of fruits and vegetables. See example below:

Complete the chart below with the fruit and vegetable plants you intend to grow in each plot of land.

## Safety & Allergies

This is a messy project! When you're working with earth or dirt you are bound to get your hands and clothes dirty, therefore provide each child with an apron, raincoat, boots and sun hat if working outdoors. Keep clothing readily accessible so you can quickly and easily have all the children ready as you start your activities. Obviously, some activities will be messier than others.

Please remember to apply ample sun cream during the hot times of the year. Allergies are another important consideration. Please ensure you have at hand a list of your students' allergies when touching and eating fruit and vegetables from *The Garden Project*.

## Timing of Activities

Every lesson plan adopts an integrated approach to learning by combining multiple disciplines into one lesson. Decide how to allocate your time to the various segments of the lesson based on the size of your group and age group you are running the activities with.

**3-4yrs**

**4-5yrs**

**5-6yrs**

### Seeds vs. Seedlings

*The Garden Project* primarily makes use of seedlings, shortening the visible vegetable life cycle and keeping students engaged throughout the growing process. If you have very limited time you can use seedlings instead of seeds, which will speed up the process. It is however important for students to grow at least one plant from a seed, as they will be able to observe the life cycle of a plant and see how a living plant grows and changes.

In addition, harvesting your own seeds from vegetable scraps or the vegetables in your Garden in the Box, is covered in the End of Year Project, and teaches children about sustainability and the cyclical nature of life, a very important lesson for them to learn!

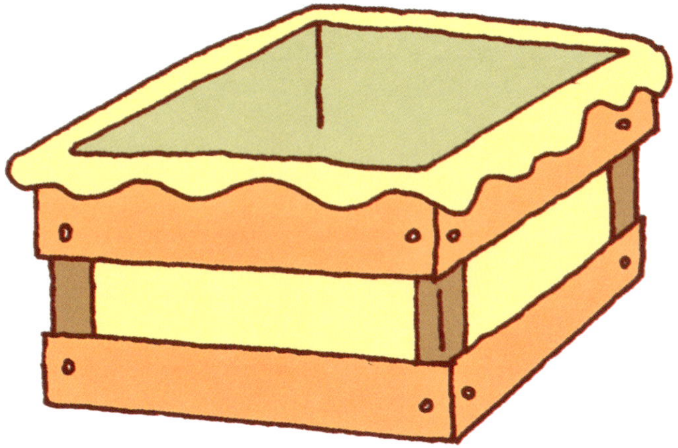

box

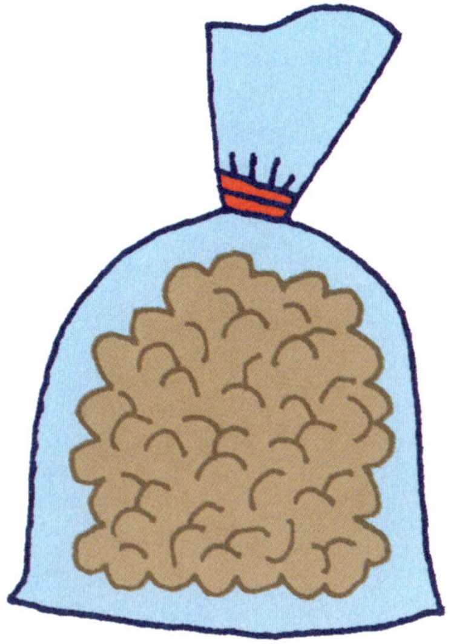

rocks/pebbles

compost/dirt

hoe

watering can

hand cultivator

trowel

**Containers and wooden crates** – 25cm deep x 50cm wide x 30cm high plastic container (with holes at the base) or wooden crates lined with a plastic bag. See Unit 2, lesson 3 for more details.

**A watering can** – plastic bottle or rain cup to water your plants. See Unit 1, lesson 4 for more details.

**Garden gloves** – to handle plant bulbs, strawberries or other fruit and vegetables that might irritate your skin.

**Canes and cane toppers** – are needed for plants that grow upwards and need support, like peas. Always use cane toppers to avoid people poking or hurting themselves accidentally.

**Compost** – Use a multipurpose compost for your plants. Don't use garden soil as it may not be the right type to help your plants grow well.

**Plant labels** – when you're planting seeds, don't forget to label them to remember what you've planted in each container. This is true for seedlings and plants. Use pictures together with the words so children can also recognize which plant the word is referring to.
See Unit 2, lesson 3 for more details.

**Trowel** – you might find a small trowel helpful for scooping up compost when you're planting or filling planters.

**Measuring tape, ruler, or string** – to measure the growth of your plants. See Unit 3, lesson 4 for more details.

**A magnifying glass** – are fabulous tools for children to observe the different parts of a plant close-up and are used throughout the project.

**Seeds, plants, vegetables, fruits** – for counting and sorting, used throughout the project.

***Cell phone*** or ***tablet*** – for children to take pictures and document the growth and changes in the plants using photographs, videos, or time-lapse technology.

**Construction paper** – for classwork and for larger projects, use construction paper that is thick enough for paint or messy work, such as the mud drawings.

**Non-toxic glue** – many of the activities require sticking beans or natural materials onto paper. Use a non-toxic glue.

**Natural dyes** – use fruits and vegetables such as strawberries, beets, or spinach as natural dyes. Red cabbage makes a fantastic dye that changes color depending on whether it is mixed with alkali or acidic substances (bicarbonate of soda, vinegar, etc).

**Mud** – the art activities proposed in *The Garden Project* are heavily influenced by the Land Art movement of the 1960s, particularly by Richard Long's work with mud. Explore mud both for its tactile qualities but also as a means to do art.

**Beans** – lots of different types of beans to shake, rattle, and roll in sound exploration!

**Containers** – containers of all sorts, to experiment with the different sounds your natural materials make whilst manipulating them in the various containers.

### Time Frame

*The Garden Project* requires preparation and planning. The flexible approach offers you the freedom to carry out *The Garden Project* at different times of the year, across a term or more extensively throughout the course of a school year. *The Garden Project* is very flexible in terms of time frames. It can be carried out at different times of year depending on your seasonality, over a semester or over the course of a school year.

If you are planning to do The Garden Project over a shorter period of time, here are some ways to save time:

- Be selective with the activities you choose to do with your students.
- Use fast-growing plants and seeds. Radishes work very well as fast-growing vegetables to observe changes, as it only takes 30-35 days from seed to radish.
- Plant seedlings from the garden center or transplant established plants.
- Use fruit and vegetables from your local market for some of the activities for healthy eating in Units 3 and 4.

## Notes

## Post-Project Reflection

What worked well about the Project? (3 things)

..........................................................................................................................

..........................................................................................................................

..........................................................................................................................

Which areas would you like to improve for next year? (3 things)

..........................................................................................................................

..........................................................................................................................

..........................................................................................................................

How can you go about preparing for next year's Garden Project?

..........................................................................................................................

..........................................................................................................................

..........................................................................................................................

..........................................................................................................................

..........................................................................................................................

..........................................................................................................................

..........................................................................................................................

..........................................................................................................................

..........................................................................................................................

..........................................................................................................................

## Families and The Garden Project

How can I involve families and carers in *The Garden Project*?

Each family will receive *The Garden Project Family Booklet*, which outlines the whole Project and what they can expect their children to learn in each of the units. Each unit also includes a suggested activity for families, carers, guardians, and grandparents to do at home with their children. There are also suggested activities to do during vacation. The family booklet should be sent home at the start of the Project to ensure parents are aware of the Project so that they can support their children's learning from home.

The Garden Project Party - Many teachers decide to invite the parents to an end of Project party, where parents have the opportunity to see all of the work and documentation that the children have done throughout the Project. It's a great opportunity to spend time outside and to prepare some lovely healthy snacks for the parents.

## Unit 1

# Preparing

*The Garden Project* follows the natural life cycle of fruit and vegetable plants from learning about the seasons and plant parts (this unit) to discovering healthy eating habits. This is the foundational unit where children learn about the elements, seasons, and parts of a plant, before getting their hands dirty and planting their own fruit and vegetable plants in the next unit.



**In this Unit:**

- Lesson 1: Season's Palette
- Lesson 2: Introduction to Plants and Plant Parts
- Lesson 3: A, B, Seeds
- Lesson 4: Reduce, Reuse, Recycle: Making Your Own Gardening Tools & Equipment

**Unit Goals**

- Understanding seasonality
- Identifying a season and its clues
- Discovering plants and parts of plants
- Learning about seeds and their roles
- Investigation of gardening tools
- Learning about recycling and finding new uses for unwanted material

# Season's Palette

*Learn about seasons and how to identify nature's clues in your environment to determine what season you're in!*

Seasonality is a concept that can be expanded upon for many weeks, although in this lesson we are introducing seasonality to awaken children's awareness of nature's clues and patterns contributing to their understanding of their environment. Seasons can easily be linked to a child's own experiences, helping them make sense of their world and immediate environment, and creating a foundation with concepts such as change, time and later the cyclicality of nature.

This lesson explores the colors of seasons as well as the feelings associated with nature and the outdoors. Children will use colors and nature's terminology to express their feelings.

Arts

Technology

Science & Nature

**Wonder**

- Season's Palette p. 6
- Today's Weather p. 7

**Observation**

- Muddy Puddles p. 6
- Season's Palette p. 7
- Outside My Window p. 8
- What's the Weather Like? p. 9

**Investigation**

- Budding Meteorologist p. 6

**Vocabulary**

sunny, rainy, windy, snowy, dry, I love..., colors, bright, light, smooth, soft, rough, furry, pointy, happy, sad

*I Love to Go Outside*, (track 2)
*The Rain Song*, (track 3)
*Sweet Corn*, (track 9)

| ACTIVITY | SKILLS | MATERIALS | JOURNALS |
|---|---|---|---|
| **Arts**<br>**All Ages**<br>• Listen to *I Love to Go Outside* and explore feelings linked with colors and the outdoors<br>• Nature walk to observe the color of nature<br>• Create a simple palette of nature's color | • *Observing colors in nature*<br>• *Learning to use the color palette*<br>• *Expressing feelings associated with the outdoors* | • The Vegetable Plot CD *I Love to Go Outside*, track 2<br>• Cardstock<br>• Color palette template<br>• Color wheel template<br>• Containers<br>• Crayons<br>**5yrs+**<br>• Empty egg cartons divided into color groups<br>• Optional: images of more than one season | W • Season's Palette p. 6<br>O • Muddy Puddles p. 6<br>• Season's Palette p. 7<br>• Outside My Window p. 8 |
| **Technology**<br>**5yrs+**<br>• Documentation of findings using photography | • *Using technology to record findings* | • Picture taking device (digital camera, smartphone, tablet) | |
| **Science & Nature**<br>**All Ages**<br>• Keeping track of the weather outside<br>**5yrs+**<br>• Making predictions about the weather | • *Developing observation skills*<br>• *Talking about the weather*<br>• *Using nature's environmental clues to promote classification (by color)* | • The Vegetable Plot CD *The Rain Song*, track 3<br>• Weather Chart | W • Today's Weather p. 7<br>O • What's the Weather Like? p.9<br>I • Budding Meteorologist p. 6 |

## Guiding Questions

**Our Green Question**
*Why is it important to know what season we're in?*

## Before and During the Lesson

- What colors are the leaves?
- Look up. What colors do you see?
- Look at the ground. What colors do you see?

## End of Lesson Reflection

- What's the weather like today?
  It is _______________ (windy/sunny/rainy/snowy/foggy).
- What season are we in?
  We are in _______________ (spring/fall/winter/summer).
- What colors can you see in (the current season)?

## Arts

*What are the colors from the season we are in?*

**All Ages**

- Start the lesson by talking about the **outdoors** and **exploring the children's emotions** about nature, seasons and the weather.

Play and **listen** to the **song** *I Love to Go Outside* (track 2) to further explore feelings.

O Talk about the **rain** and ask children to **document** their feelings of rainy weather by completing the *Muddy Puddles* activity on page 6.

- *What colors make up the season we're in? How do colors change? What colors are the leaves? What colors do you see? (in the sky/on the ground/ at eye level)? What season are we in?* Prepare to **go on a nature walk**. It is not necessary to go far, you can go to the **school garden** or a **local park**. If this is not possible, ask children to collect items (as detailed below) on their way to or from school or take pictures of some nature items they find on a nature walk.

- Ask children to **collect four items from the ground** and put them in a container. Items have to be **natural materials** they find on the ground (smooth with no rough edges that could hurt them in any way) and respectful of nature as much as possible.

- Repeat this activity to **observe colors** at eye level and later in the sky by looking up without looking directly at the sun.

W O Capture these colors by asking the children to **shade** their **palettes** with the colors they found on their walk on the *Season's Palette* activity (Wonder p. 6, Observation p. 7).

O Once children have their color palette, ask them to draw a picture using the colors they observed on their walk and **draw a tree** in the **colors** they saw in their natural environment on *Outside My Window* on page 8 of their journal.

**Teacher's Tips**

Children might find it difficult to notice the colors of natural materials and cues, often being drawn to bright colored man-made objects in their surroundings. To facilitate the activity, take a small piece of cardstock the size of a business card, and punch a small hole in the middle to create a "pinhole camera". This will help children isolate and identify colors as they're looking at nature.

## Technology

*What devise can we use to help us identify colors in nature? How do the colors change on our devise?*

**5yrs+**

- Ask children to take **photos** of four items they find on their nature walk, found at different levels (ground, eye level, trees and sky) and ask the students to **arrange** the photographs by **colors and shades**.

## Science & Nature

*What season are we in?*
*What is the weather like in (the current season)?*

### All Ages

Now **discuss** the weather. *What's the weather like today?* Ask children what their favorite type of weather is and play *The Rain Song* (track 3) to talk about the rain and the sun.

All plants need some rain or sun to grow. Ask children to **document** the weather in *Today's Weather* (Wonder, p. 7) and *What's the Weather Like?* (Observation, p. 9).

Ask the children to recall yesterday's weather or make predictions about tomorrow's weather. Complete the findings on the *Budding Meteorologist* chart on page 6 of the journal.

## Project Ideas

- Explore local seasonal festivals and traditions. A well-known example is the *"Festa Junina"*, or June Festival, and is related to the seasonal corn harvest.

- Explore the colors of textures of the harvest and the festival and then hold your own mini-festival with seasonal food such as corn on the cob, popcorn and *"pamonha"*, a traditional Brazilian food made from corn puree wrapped in corn husks. Play the song *Sweet Corn* (track 9) from The Vegetable Plot CD.

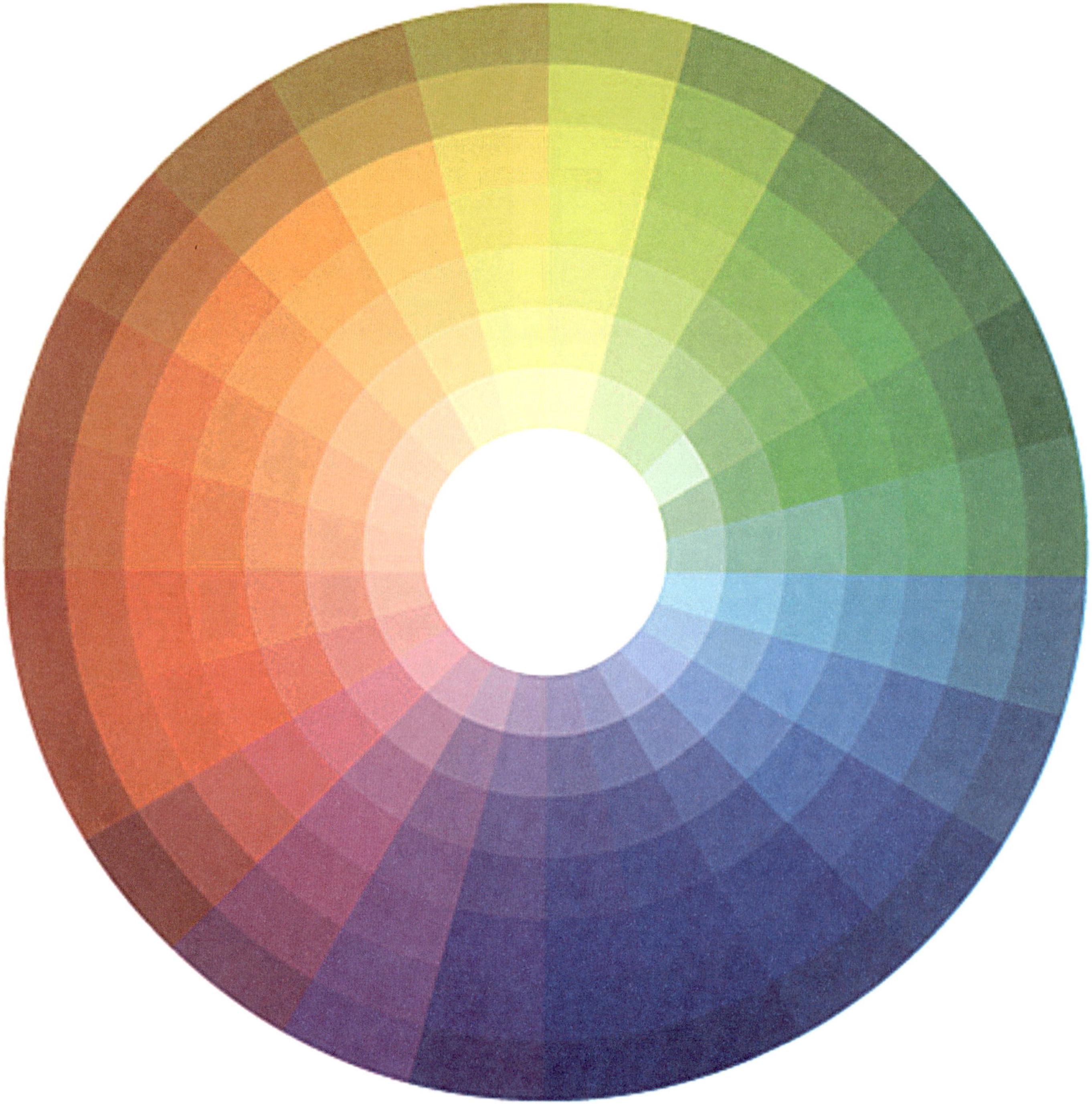

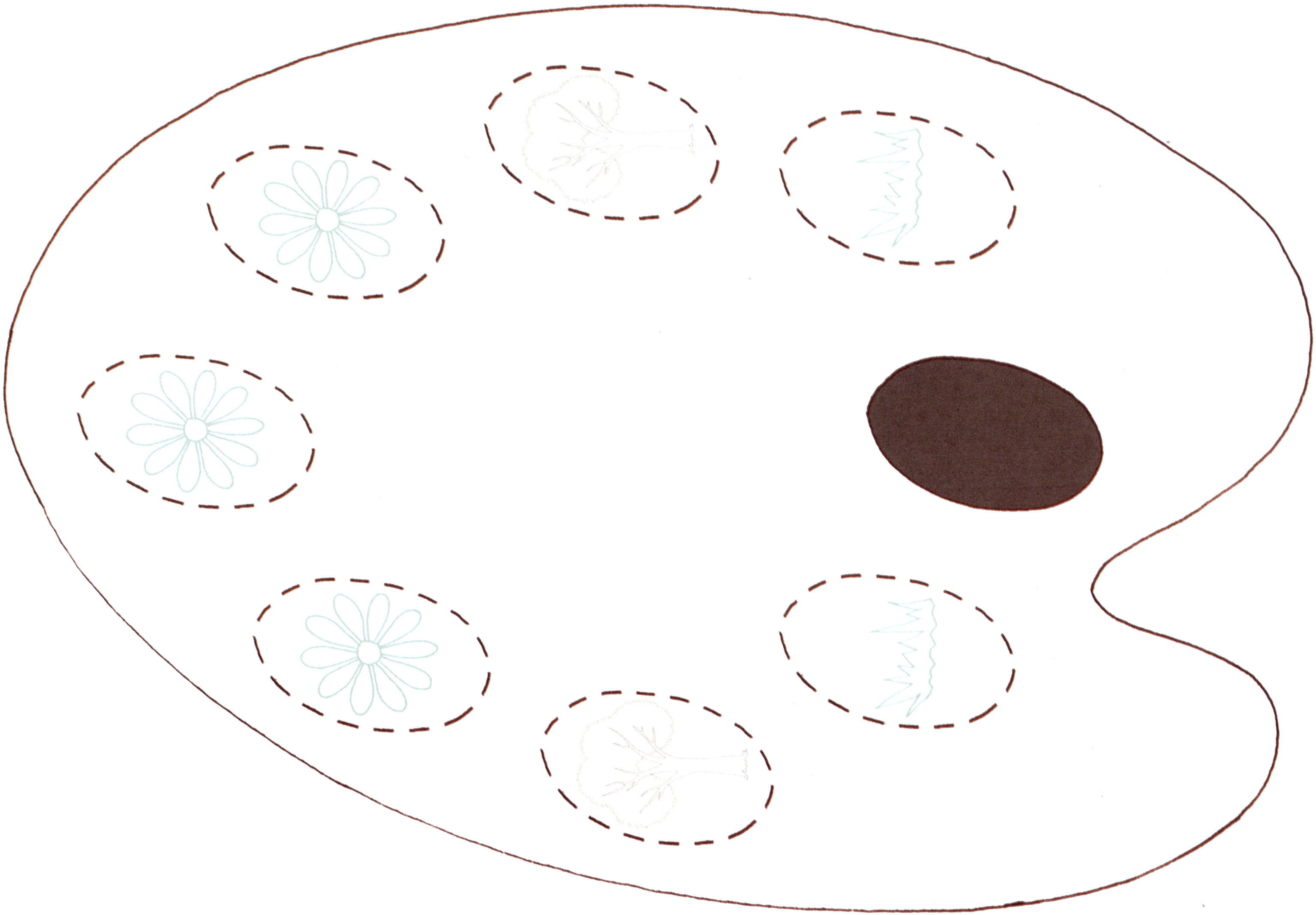

# TODAY'S WEATHER

# Introduction to Plants and Plant Parts

*Learn about the different plant parts, each with its own special function(s).*

This lesson takes children on an exploration of plants, identifying them as living things, examining the parts of plants and giving them an understanding of what plants need to live and grow. They will nurture and appreciate the importance of plants and other living things.

**Science & Nature** **Engineering** **Arts**

**W** **Wonder**
- Leaves, Leaves, Everywhere p. 8
- Flower Garden p. 9
- Leaves and Seasons p. 10
- Forest of Leaves p. 11

**O** **Observation**
- Root Drawing p. 10
- Leaves, Leaves, Everywhere p. 11
- Patterns of Leaves pp. 12-13

**I** **Investigation**
- Root Drawing p. 7
- Leaf Insect p. 8

**Vocabulary**
seed(s), stem, leaves, roots, sun, small, grow, big, plant, water, quietly

*Under the Ground Organic,* (track 13)

| ACTIVITY | SKILLS | MATERIALS | JOURNALS |
|---|---|---|---|
| **Science & Nature**<br>**All Ages**<br>• Demonstration and identification of the parts of a plant<br>• Identification of the parts of a plant through dance and songs<br>• Observation of parts of a plant using a magnifying glass<br>**4yrs+**<br>• Representation of roots using ink, a straw and blowing the ink in different directions | • *Identifying and classifying flora*<br>• *Observing parts of plants*<br>• *Developing fine motor skills through the use of a magnifying glass and straws* | • One or more potted plants with developed root systems<br>• Seeds<br>• Magnifying glasses<br>• Sample of each part of a plant: leaf, root, stem, flower, fruit, seeds, bulb<br>**4yrs+**<br>• Ink, 1 or 2 colors<br>• The Vegetable Plot CD *Under the Ground Organic*, track 13 | W • Leaves, Leaves, Everywhere p. 8<br>O • Root Drawing p. 10<br>I • Root Drawing p. 7 |
| **Engineering**<br>**5yrs+**<br>• Experimentation with a celery stalk and blue food coloring to see how liquid moves from the roots up | • *Demonstrating how plants get their food up to their leaves* | • Cardboard tubes (from paper towel, for example)<br>• Balls that can easily roll up and down the cardboard tube<br>• Magnifying glasses<br>• 1 celery stalk per small group<br>• 1 clear container (or cup) of water per group or shared.<br>• Blue food coloring (several drops per container) | |
| **Arts**<br>**3-4yrs**<br>• Visual exploration of flowers with simple lines and squiggles<br>• Use of poster paint, cork and printing techniques to complete the leaves and flowers on a tree<br>**4yrs+**<br>• Identification of different leaf shapes | • *Visually representing parts of a plant (flower/ roots/ leaves)*<br>• *Developing a sense of imagination by using parts of a plant to create compositional and representational drawings* | **3yrs+**<br>• Crayons (blue, red, yellow)<br>• Leaves<br>• Glue<br>• Poster paint (colors vary according to the season, for example, green, orange, yellow, brown)<br>• Corks, 2 per child<br>• Plates for paint<br>**4yrs+**<br>• Ink pad<br>• Leaves<br>• Glue | W • Flower Garden p. 9<br>• Leaves and Seasons p. 10<br>• Forest of Leaves p. 11<br>O • Leaves, Leaves, Everywhere p. 11<br>• Patterns of Leaves pp. 12-13<br>I • Leaf Insect p. 8 |

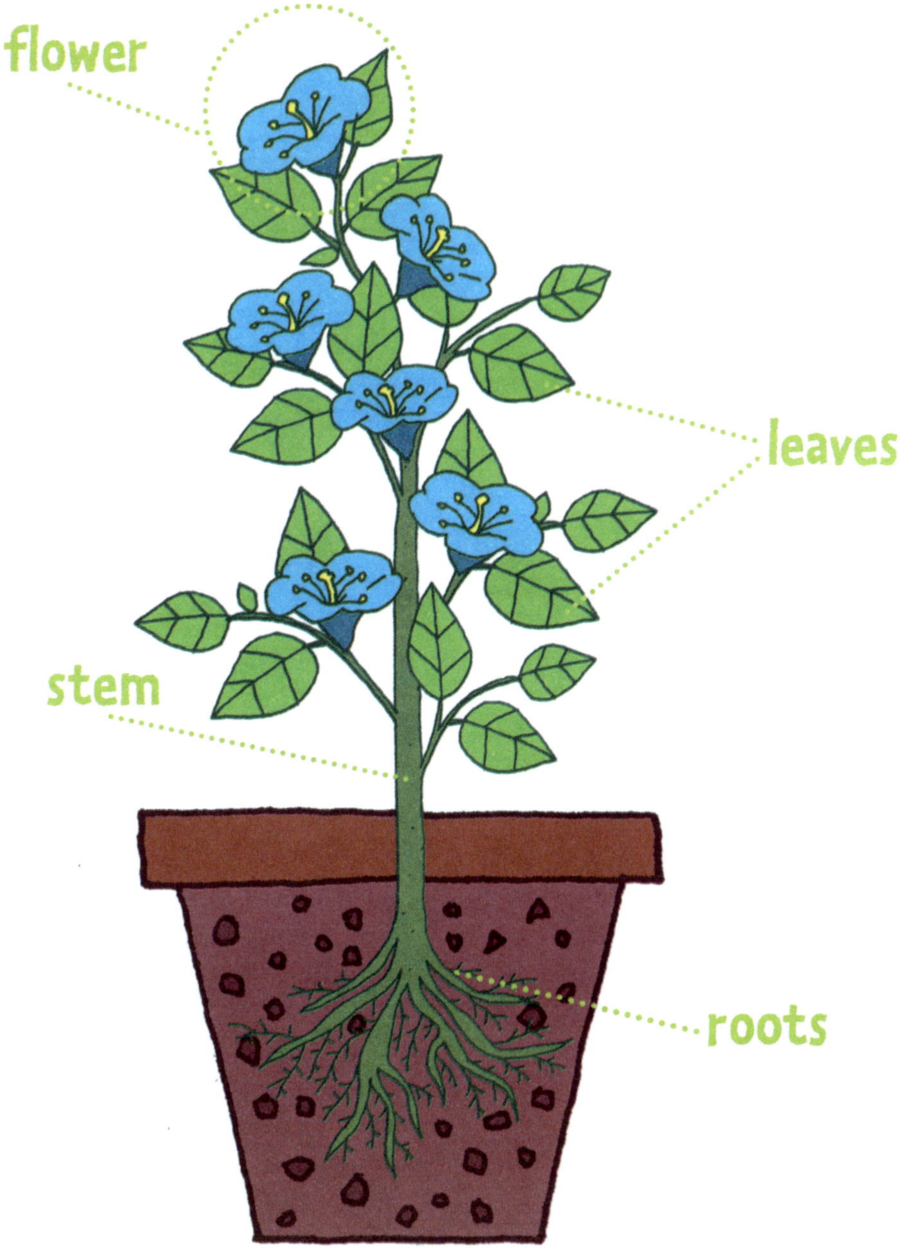


## Guiding Questions

**Our Green Question**
*Why does a plant have different parts?*

## Before and During the Lesson

- What are the roots and leaves for? What is the stem for?
- Can you see the veins in the leaves?
- Look at two different plants. Do they have the same parts?

## End of Lesson Reflection

- How does a plant get its food from the roots to the leaves?
- What are the roots for? What are the stem and leaves for?
- Look at a tree. Can you see the trunk and the roots?

## Science & Nature

*Can you name the main parts of a plant?*

### Teacher Set-Up

- Before the lesson, loosen the potted plant from the sides of the pot so that you can remove it easily to show the plant's root system. Sit down again and bring the children's attention to the plant. Show them the plant you've brought in.

**All Ages**

- **Identify the parts of the plant** and associate them with body parts. For example, roots can be associated with feet, stem with the torso and the children's hands could be the "leaves", fingers are "flowers". **Stand up and act out** growing big, repeat several times varying the speed of growth (slowly and quickly).

Parts of the Plants
(Sung to: "Head, Shoulders, Knees and Toes")

Do you know the parts of plants, parts of plants?
Do you know the parts of plants, parts of plants?
All kinds of plants that grow and grow and grow.
Do you know the parts of plants, parts of plants?

The roots hold the plant in place, plant in place.
(crouch down and touch your feet as you sing "roots")
The stem moves food up the plant, up the plant.
(glide your hands from your feet, up your legs up to your chest)
The leaves soak up the sun.
(hold your hands out and wiggle your fingers)
The flower grows into fruit, into fruit.
(hold your fists in front of you and gradually open)

**Play** and **dance** to the **song** *Under the Ground Organic* (track 13) as children identify their roots and stems to the beat of the music.

- Now examine the plant(s) you have brought. Start by examining the **leaves** of the plant. **What are leaves for?** Explain that the leaves use light from the sun, to make food for the plant. Point out the veins of a leaf and explain that the plant's food gets transported through its veins. Then turn the children's attention to the stem. Introduce the word **stem. What is the stem for?** Explain that the stem helps hold the plant up and carries water and food (nutrients) from the roots to the other parts of the plant. **Gently pull the plant from the pot** and brush the dirt away from the roots. Introduce the word **roots. What are the roots for?** Explain that roots absorb water and food from the soil.

- Hand out the **magnifying glasses** and ask the children to **examine** the parts of the plant closely. When looking at leaves, some veins are easy to see because they are bigger, like in a cabbage leaf. *Can you see the veins in the leaves?* Encourage the children to examine the roots with magnifying glasses. Focus their attention on the tiny root hairs at the ends of the roots.

- Look at two different plants. *Do they have the same parts?*

W Ask children to identify the shapes and veins on a leaf by tracing the leaves with their fingers using the *Leaves, Leaves, Everywhere* drawings on page 8 of their journal.

O Children complete the root system of the *Root Drawing* on page 10 of their journal.

I Children focus their attention on the elaborate root system, attempting to fill the page with as many roots as possible on the *Root Drawing* on page 7 of their journal.

### Engineering

*How can you show how water travels up the stem to the leaves?*

**5yrs+**

- **Investigate** how a plant's food travels to the leaves or branches through its stem by **handing** a ball and a cardboard tube to children and asking them if they can make the ball go up the tube without tipping the tube upside-down. Difficult, isn't it?! *Are the cardboard tubes similar to the stems? If so, how? How are they different?* Make the analogy with trees and plants and how they can bring food all the way up through their stems, starting from their roots up.

- Have some **celery stalks** available with **one cup of water** and **blue food coloring**. If possible, in small groups distribute one celery stalk per child, having children observe the celery stalk. *What color are the celery stalks?* Children can use a magnifying **glass** to notice the tubes in the stalk (the white part, at the base of the stalk).

- Next put four drops of **blue food coloring** in the water and put the celery stalk in the water. Leave the stalks to soak in the blue water for at least four hours or overnight. Now ask the children to observe their celery stalks. *What color are the celery stalks now? How far has the blue water moved up the stalk? Are some celery stalks more blue than others? Why?*

### Arts

*How can we show the parts of a plant or tree on paper?*

**All Ages**

- Explore the different parts of a plant visually and use your imagination to see things differently.

W **Visually explore** flowers by using spirals and lines in bright colors. Complete the *Flower Garden* on page 9 in the journal with squiggles, spirals, and lines. Next, ask children to complete the leaves of the tree on *Leaves and Seasons*, page 10, by dipping the cork tops into paint and then printing them onto the page to represent a tree in its environment.

Go **on a nature walk** and ask children to **collect** some leaves and use them to make a **compositional representation** of a forest on the *Forest of Leaves* on page 11 of their journal.

O Children visually **represent** the veins **of a leaf** they observe by pressing the leaf on the **ink pad** (dab if it's delicate) and **printing** it on *Leaves, Leaves, Everywhere* on page 11 of their journal. They then complete the *Patterns of Leaves* on pages 12 and 13.

I Use leaves to build children's imagination with the *Leaf Insect* on page 8 by **gluing leaves** to form a compositional drawing.

## Observations

# A, B, Seeds

*Developing early math skills through the classification of seeds.*

Children will examine seeds up close and discover that there are a variety of types of seeds, in this case beans, and sort them. In addition, they will have a tactile exploration of bumpy and smooth, big and small seeds (beans).

**Arts**

**Math**

**Wonder**
- Sunflower p. 12
- Bean Art p. 13

**Observation**
- Spill the Beans pp. 14-15
- A, B, Seeds! pp. 16-17

**Vocabulary**
seeds, bean, grow, plant, water, shake, small, big, round, smooth, bumpy

*Little Green Heads,* (track 5)

| ACTIVITY | SKILLS | MATERIALS | JOURNALS |
|---|---|---|---|
| **Arts**<br>**All Ages**<br>• Tactile and sound exploration of beans in containers<br><br>**3yrs+**<br>• Development of fine motor skills by tracing circles and loops in a tray of lentils<br><br>**4yrs+**<br>• Tactile exploration of seeds through the seed Memory game<br><br>**3-4yrs**<br>• Creation of compositional drawings using beans | **3yrs**<br>• *Developing fine motor movements and skills*<br><br>**All Ages**<br>• *Developing a steady beat*<br>• *Developing attentive listening skills*<br>• *Identifying tactile differences of beans*<br>• *Developing visual arts through compositional drawings and patterns repetition* | **3yrs+**<br>• Lentils<br>• Sunflower seeds<br><br>**4yrs+**<br>• Variety of beans (seeds) of different shapes and color: lentils, red kidney beans, black beans, chickpeas and fava bean<br>• White glue<br><br>**All Ages**<br>• 3 lined tubs, one lined with cloth, the second with aluminum foil and the third with plastic<br>• 2 small plastic bottles per child<br>• The Vegetable Plot CD, *Little Green Heads*, track 5 | W • Sunflower p. 12<br>• Bean Art p. 13<br><br>O • Spill the Beans pp. 14-15 |
| **Math**<br>**4yrs+**<br>• Categorization of different beans | • *Sorting, graphing, counting, reading a bar graph* | • Variety of beans (seeds) in different shapes and colors – such as lentils, red kidney beans, black beans, etc<br>• Ice trays<br>• Plastic bottles with lines around them | O • A, B, Seeds! pp. 16-17 |

## Guiding Questions

> **Our Green Question**
> *How are seeds different?*

## Before and During the Lesson

- Are the seeds big or small?
- What colors are the seeds?
- What sounds do they make (when shaken in a bottle)?

## End of Lesson Reflection

- What happens when you put a seed in the ground?
- How are seeds the same?
- How are seeds different?

## Arts

> *How can you explore the different textures and patterns of seeds? What differences do you notice in the seeds? What do the seeds feel like? (smooth, bumpy, round, big, small).*

- **Review** what the children have already learned about plants and plant parts, connecting it to seeds.

**3-5yrs**

- Hand out one tray per child/small group and **pour lentils** onto it so that they can practice **making finger drawings** in the lentils. Instruct children to make **loops** and **circles** in their trays.

**4yrs+**

- **Gather a variety of bean seeds**, such as lentils, red kidney beans, black beans, etc. The more they vary in size, the better. **Distribute** different types and sizes of beans, making sure each child gets a variety of beans.

- Remind children that they must not eat these. Divide the children into pairs and ask them to **explore the textures and sizes of the beans** by playing a tactile memory game. One child has to choose four beans of different sizes and the other child has to **feel the beans with their eyes closed**. The child who had their eyes closed has to select the beans from the pile **guessing which types they felt**. How many did you get right? Now change and the other child guesses the beans.

**All Ages**

- Once children have completed the tactile exploration, move to the **exploration of** sounds. Ask them to **pour** their **seeds** into **three different tubs**: one lined with fabric, another with aluminum and the third with plastic and explore the sounds. What sounds do they make? Distribute **two small plastic bottles** to each child/small group and ask the children to fill the plastic bottles with the different types of beans. Children aged 4yrs and up should sort between the two containers based on the size of the seed. Screw the caps on the bottles firmly and ask the children to shake the bottles – down low and up high – and explore the **sounds** they make. Do the two bottles sound the same?

- One way of exploring sound in plastic bottles is to use the bottle as a guiro (a type of percussion instrument) using a stick and scraping it against the plastic ridges of the bottle.

Introduce the ***Little Green Heads*** song first by singing it together and then by shaking your instruments to the beat. Repeat the lyrics several times. You can do this as a chant first. Once the children have learned the words, play them the song (track 5).

W **Distribute 10-20 sunflower seeds** to each child and ask them to glue their seeds onto the *Sunflower* on page 12 of their journal. Next pour the lentils or other beans on a tray to complete the *Bean Art* on page 13. Use white or light-colored beans to create a more beautiful composition.

O Pour the beans out of the containers into the central rectangle on *Spill the Beans*, pages 14 and 15, and finish the composition by asking the children to place their beans on the dotted lines.

## Math

*How can you group the seeds by shape/color/size? How are the seeds similar/different? What is the smallest/largest seed?*

**4yrs+**

- Distribute ice trays, one per child/small group and ask the children to pour the beans on the table so that they can sort the beans into the containers by bean type (shape, color or size).

Ask children to complete the bean sorting bar graph *A, B, Seeds!* on pages 16 and 17 of the journal by placing each bean in its category. For a further challenge, children can try naming the beans.

## Observations

# Reduce, Reuse, Recycle: Making Your Own Gardening Tools & Equipment

*Use your creativity to reduce, reuse, and recycle in your classroom and your garden!*

In this lesson, children will discover the equipment needed to facilitate gardening and manipulation of natural materials. The most obvious is a watering can to water plants, but also shovels, trowels, and rakes.

This lesson focuses on reusing and repurposing materials so that they can be reused in a different context (upcycling). Children will recycle plastic bottles and paper cups to reuse them as watering equipment and use yogurt pots as plant pots. In this way, children learn the importance, not only of caring for each other, but also of caring for nature and the environment that surrounds them.

**Engineering**

**Vocabulary**
water, cup, bottle, seeds, dirt, fill, sprinkle, hole, pour

*The Rain Song,* (track 3)

| ACTIVITY | SKILLS | MATERIALS | JOURNALS |
| --- | --- | --- | --- |
| **Engineering**<br>**All Ages**<br>• Conversion of old plastic water bottles and paper cups to make watering devices<br><br>**Project Ideas**<br>**All Ages**<br>Conversion of yogurt pots into plant pots | • *Finding different uses for everyday materials*<br>• *Manipulating water with various materials*<br>• *Investigating water regulation by perforating holes into materials*<br>• *Promoting sustainable practices*<br>• *Applying "upcycling" practices by finding a new purpose for an old item* | • Sample watering can, (shovel, trowel, rake are optional) to show children<br>• Old plastic bottles with a hole in the caps or caps with a nozzle (one per child or small group)<br>• Scissors for the teacher<br>• Old paper cups, with and without holes in the base (one of each, per child or small group)<br>• Washing-up bowls filled with water<br>• Unwanted household/classroom items to upcycle, such as yogurt pots<br>• The Vegetable Plot CD, *The Rain Song*, track 3 | |

## Guiding Questions

**Our Green Question**
*Why is it important to use old materials in a new way?*

## Before and During the Lesson

- Plants need water. How do plants get water in nature?
- Think about indoor plants. How can we give them water?
- Look at the watering can. How can we make our cups or bottles like the watering can?

## End of Lesson Reflection

- How did we change the bottle/cup?
- Can plants have too much water?
- Look around the classroom. Can you see any other objects we can reuse or 'upcycle'? How do we need to change it?

**Engineering**

*How can we reuse (upcycle) old paper cups and plastic bottles to water our plants?*

- Find out how many of the children have already planted or gardened before. Discuss gardening equipment and show children a watering can. You can show them other equipment such as a trowel or a shovel if you have them. We need these tools to help plant our garden and take care of it.

Ask children how nature waters plants. *What does rain sound like?* Ask children to mimic loud heavy rain and quiet soft rain with their fingertips. **Play** *The Rain Song* (track 3) from The Vegetable Plot CD and have students sing along with the chorus.

- Explain that plants need not too much, not too little, but just the right amount of water. *What if there's no rain or the plants are indoors? How can we give them water?*

- Using the watering can as an example, ask the children if there are **other items** in the **room** they could use to transport water. Remind the children that you don't always have to throw trash away. Whenever possible you should find new ways to reuse old items to reduce waste.

- Next show them an old, empty **water bottle**. *Look at the bottle. What's it for? Is the hole of the bottle big or small?* Let the children give you their suggestions and then hand an empty bottle of water to each child or small group. Pour some water from the bottle.

- Now show them a **paper cup** (without holes in it). Look at the cup. *What's it for? Is the hole of the cup big or small?* Ask a child to pour water from the cup.

- **Organize** children into **smaller groups** working around a **washing-up bowl**. Let the children **play** with the **water**. Remind them that they must keep the water in the washing-up bowl and not on the floor.

Encourage children to fill bottles and cups up and empty them out into the washing-up bowl. *Does the water come out faster from the bottle or the cup?*

- *Does more water come out of the bottle or the cup?*

- Now look at the watering can. Demonstrate. *Does the water come out fast or slow? What can we observe from where the water comes out? Is there one big hole? Are the holes big or small?* Explain that a watering can sprinkles water and this helps us give plants the right amount.

- *How can we make our bottles and cups more like a watering can?* Accept different ideas. Distribute **plastic lids with holes** in them and ask children to screw them onto the plastic bottles. Then, give out cups with holes in them. Now ask them to use their bottles to **squirt water** out and experiment **regulating** different amounts of water. Children should be experimenting by **pouring water** from water bottles into the cups with holes in them so that eventually they've devised a way to **sprinkle** plants with water.

**5yrs+**
- Children can further **investigate** ways in which they can **regulate** the flow of water from their cups. Under adult supervision/with assistance, children poke holes in the bottom of their cups with a ballpoint pen.

## Project Ideas

**All Ages**
- Explore the concept of **reusing** (upcycling) old materials for **plant** pots. Repurposed plant pots can include: yogurt pots, large plastic bottles, old rain boots, old egg cartons and even egg shells!

**5yrs+**
- *What other gardening tools do you need for your garden? Can you reuse (upcycle) anything else that you no longer have use for?*

## Observations

# Unit 2
# Planting

The Garden Project provides your children with the opportunity to experience life processes first-hand. In this unit children will learn that getting your hands dirty is fun and is the first step to having a budding green thumb. Children will have a better understanding of the world we live in by observing plants from up close and gain a deeper appreciation for plants as living organisms.

**In this Unit:**

- Lesson 1: Let's Get Dirty!
- Lesson 2: Companion Planting
- Lesson 3: Planting the Garden in the Box
- Lesson 4: Friends of the Garden

**Unit Goals**

- Learning to get our hands dirty
- Identifying different types of soils
- Understanding the difference between plants' needs
- Understanding that plants are "producers" and make food for us
- Planting the Garden in the Box
- Identifying creatures that are friends or pests
- Understanding the balance in nature

# Let's Get Dirty!

*Creative expression through mud paintings.*

In this activity, children explore soil, mud, and sand (natural materials) and their texture and are introduced to the Land Art movement and Abstract Expressionism.

Research shows that children who spend time playing and getting dirty outdoors lead healthier and happier lives. In fact, experts state that playing in the dirt even helps children build stronger immune systems. (Dr. M. Ruebush)

**Science & Nature**

**Arts**

**W** **Wonder**
- Muddy Print p. 14

**O** **Observation**
- Mud Drawings p. 18

**Vocabulary**
soil, water, mix, mud, puddle, walk, look, circle, thick, dry, moist, smooth, soft, wet, sand, lumpy, cold, warm, light

**5yrs+**
*I Love to Go Outside,*
(track 2)

| ACTIVITY | SKILLS | MATERIALS | JOURNALS |
|---|---|---|---|
| **Science & Nature**<br>**All Ages**<br>• Feel the difference in textures between sand, soil, and mud | • *Identifying the role and uses of soil in nature*<br>• *Describing the differences in texture between soil, sand, and mud* | • 6 containers per group (2 for sand, 2 for soil, 2 for mud)<br>• Water<br>• Soil (potting mix)<br>• Sand<br>• Mud (optional) | |
| **Arts**<br>**All Ages**<br>• Introduction to Land Art and the use of mud in drawing<br>• Experimentation with water and soil to make different shades of mud | • *Developing hand-eye coordination*<br>• *Developing creativity through messy play*<br>• *Moving to a steady beat* | • Soil or mud<br>• Water<br>**5yrs+**<br>• Card, one piece per child<br>• The Vegetable Plot CD, *I Love to Go Outside*, track 2 | W • Muddy Print p. 14<br>O • Mud Drawings p. 18 |

## Guiding Questions

**Our Green Question**
*Why do different types of soil feel different?*

## Before and During the Lesson

- (Introduce each of the three natural materials) What's this? What does it look like?
- Where can you find sand/soil/mud outside?
- How do they (sand/soil/mud) feel different?

## End of Lesson Reflection

- Can you describe sand/soil/mud?
- What texture do you like the most? Why?
- Which natural material should we choose for our garden?

## Science & Nature

*How are the textures of sand, soil, and mud different?*

### All Ages

- Soil is a mixture of water, air, organic matter, food (minerals), and decaying remains of plants, leaves, and other organisms. It is the "*skin of the earth*" and is what gives plants life and food.

- Prepare **6 containers with 2 matching textures**: 2 with sand, 2 with soil (potting soil) and 2 with mud (mud from the outdoors, ensuring there are no sharp objects in it like rocks, or soil mixed with water). **Cover 3 of the containers** (i.e. 1 sand, 1 dirt, and 1 mud container). *Where can you find sand/soil/mud outside?*

- Position the other 3 containers in front of the children and ask them to **feel inside the covered containers** and **describe** their **textures** and **find** the **matching tray**. *What does sand/soil/mud feel like? How does sand feel different to mud? How does soil feel different to mud?*

## Arts

*What happens to the color and texture of soil if you add water?*

### All Ages

- Prepare a 50cm x 50cm box of soil before **talking** about **rain** and its **sounds**. Encourage children to practice making **"shh" sounds**, to replicate the sound of the rain.

- Choose a **large space**, ideally the outdoors. Allow children to **play** with the **soil**. Not all children will feel comfortable manipulating the soil or mud, so allow each child to manipulate soil in their own time. Children **mix soil and water** with their fingers to create mud and make **different consistencies of mud**, observing their different shades of brown. Assist as needed.

- To lighten the color of mud simply add more water and to make it darker add more soil.

W — Children experiment with mud on their feet and make the *Muddy Prints* on page 14 of their journals.

O — Ask the students to dip their fingers in the mud and paint a handprint on the *Mud Drawings* activity, page 18 of their journal.

### 5yrs+

- Children can **apply mud** to the surface of **thick card** to make works of art that can be hung in the classroom.

Play ***I Love to Go Outside***, track 2 of The Vegetable Plot CD. Ask the children about what the mud feels like. Explore tactile sensations of mud: soft, moist, wet, cold, warm.

**Teacher's Tips**

This activity is inspired by the Land Art movement (also known as earthworks or Earth Art) where natural elements found in nature are used as the principal materials. These include rock, soil, leaves, water, and tree branches. In this way, the art becomes part of the landscape and the landscape becomes part of the art.

## Observations

# Companion Planting

*Exploring and understanding the concept of cooperation and collaboration through plants.*

As we prepare to plant our Garden in the Box or in our outside garden, children learn that some plants can keep other plants healthy if they are growing close by. This is called *companion planting. Companion planting* refers to the concept of planting two different plants or crops close to each other. There are many benefits to companion planting including: pest control, pollination, providing habitats, and maximizing crop productivity.

Companion planting is a great way to introduce collaboration and friendship to children. Just like plants, some children naturally tend to complement each other and work better together than others.

**Science & Nature**

**Arts**

**Observation**
- My Companion Plants p. 19

**Vocabulary**
friends, vegetable names (customize according to the list of vegetables you have selected), combinations, work well, get along, companion

| ACTIVITY | SKILLS | MATERIALS | JOURNALS |
|---|---|---|---|
| **Science & Nature**<br>**All Ages**<br>• Discussion about friendships and introduction to the concept of companion planting<br>**4yrs+**<br>• Identification and association of plants with their companion(s) | • *Pattern combinations using plants* | **4yrs+**<br>• Vegetable cut-outs from pages 80 and 81; and garden marker templates from pages 82 and 83<br>• Colored pencils<br>• Card<br>• Glue | 0 • My Companion Plants p. 19 |
| **Arts**<br>**4yrs+**<br>• Visual representation of the link between companion planting and collaboration by grouping children through their common interests and planting a photograph/picture in a cardboard pot | • *Linking pattern awareness with complementary colors* | • Four passport-sized photographs of children or pieces of card to draw portraits<br>• 10 or more small cardboard plant pots (ideally one per child)<br>• Labels or garden markers<br>• Markers<br>• Wooden sticks<br>• Glue | |

## Guiding Questions

**Our Green Question**
*Why do plants have plant friends?*

## Before and During the Lesson

- What is a friend?
- Do you have a friend you play well with?
- Do you think plants have friends too?

## End of Lesson Reflection

- Can you name two plants that are friends?
- Can you name three plants that are friends?
- Can you name two (or more) plants that aren't friends?

## Science & Nature

*Which plants are friends? Which plants aren't friends?*

### All Ages

- *What is a friend? Do you have a friend you play well with? Do you think plants have friends too?*
- *Why do you think plants grow better if planted near their friends?* Companion planting is based on the principle that some plants work better together than others and by planting them next to each other they will grow healthier and produce more vegetables. For example, if you have a plant that needs pollinators to make its fruit, you can put a plant that attracts pollinators next to it, to *companion plant*.

- Take a look at these **good plant combinations**:

- Some fruit and vegetables **don't like to be planted together** at all, for example:

Turn to the *My Companion Plants* activity on page 19 of the journal and complete the garden marker with a picture of the fruit or vegetable that was planted and a picture of a plant that likes to be planted next to it in the bottom right corner of the marker.

### 5yrs+

- Photocopy the cut-outs of fruit and vegetables on pages 80 and 81 and ask the children to **cut out** and **combine** two or more plants that work well together and **glue** these onto card.

- Next, photocopy the *Garden Markers* templates on pages 82 and 83 so that each child can complete a garden marker with their chosen fruit or vegetable. Be sure that the template used matches its companion plant. If you don't find a companion plant, create your own using the blank template. Keep and use these markers for the next lesson, when you plant your Garden in the Box.

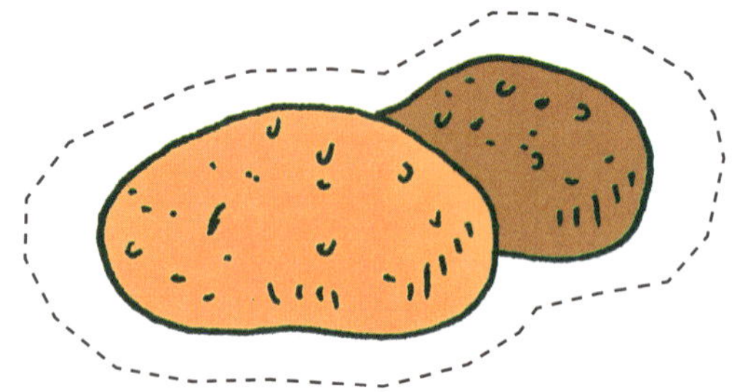

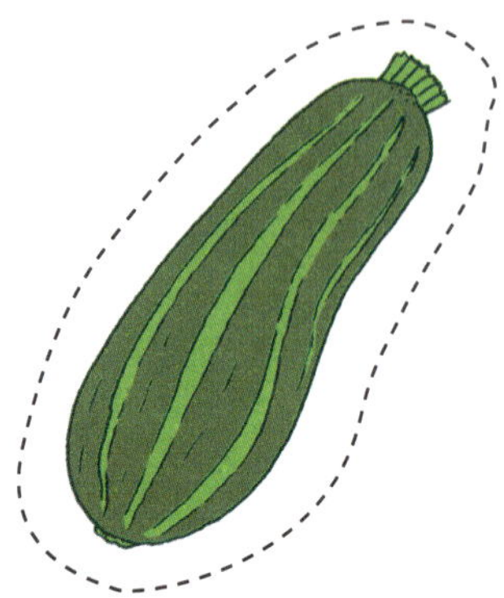

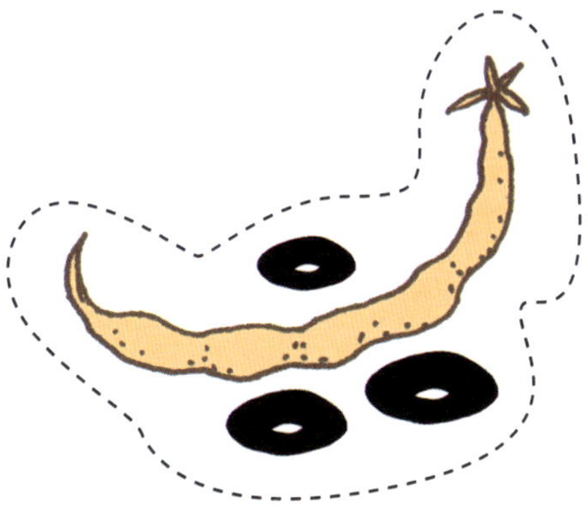

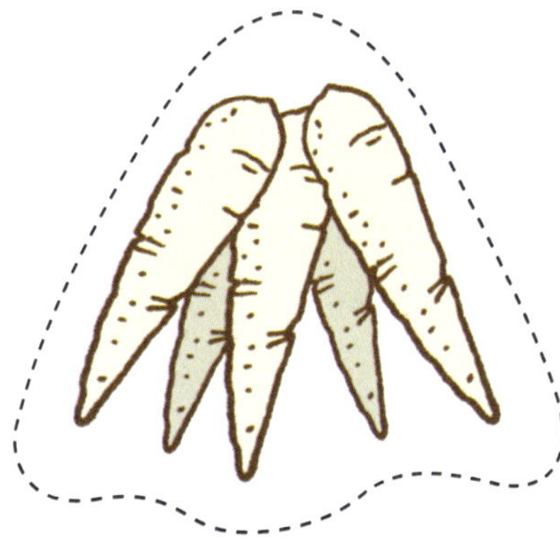

________________ plant

________________ plant

________________ plant

________________ plant

__________________ plant

__________________ plant

__________________ plant

__________________ plant

Arts

4yrs+

- Ask children to bring **four passport-sized pictures** of themselves each, printed on paper. Alternatively, they can **draw self-portraits**. Set up four "corners of interest" and ask children to go to the corner they like best. Once they are naturally grouped into their corners of interest, give them **wooden sticks to glue their photos/drawings** to and add themselves to the little plant pots, having them notice how some friends share common interests. Name each corner of interest with "Companion Planting and [name of the corner of interest]".

## Observations

# Planting the Garden in the Box

*Create your **Garden in the Box** with seedlings and small vegetable plants. Watch it grow!*

Gardening skills such as planting provide fabulous ways for children to refine fine motor skills as well as teach them an incredibly important life skill: patience. In this section, children will learn about the basic elements a plant needs to grow: soil (nutrients), rain and sun, and a lot of care.

In this lesson, we will give you the step-by-step process to create your mini-edible **Garden in the Box** out of your cardboard box, wooden crate, or plastic box and teach children the vocabulary to go with it. Choosing small plants allows children to see the process without losing interest and delight in eating their home-grown produce!

Grouping four to five children to work on a box together is a very powerful experience as children start to recognize the importance of collaboration as well as "personal space" needed in this activity. Plants also need space to grow, just like people.

Science & Nature

Arts

Technology

**Wonder**
- Little Green Heads p. 15

**Observation**
- Little Green Heads p. 20

**Investigation**
- Garden in the Box p. 9
- Plant Me pp. 10-11

**Vocabulary**
the names of the fruit and vegetable plants you choose for your garden.
planting, growing, seeds, stem, leaves

*Little Green Heads,*
(track 5)

| ACTIVITY | SKILLS | MATERIALS | JOURNALS |
| --- | --- | --- | --- |
| **Arts**<br>**5yrs+**<br>• Preparation for gardening by planning and completing the plot template | • *Visually planning and designing a garden* | • Card, one piece per child<br>OR<br>• Vegetable plot template on page 87<br>• Black markers<br>• Colored pens or pencils | |
| **Science & Nature**<br>**All Ages**<br>• Plant the *Garden in the Box* by filling your cardboard box, wooden or plastic crate with potting soil and planting 5 small vegetable plants in it<br>• Alternatively, plant in the school garden | • *Developing fine motor skills through transplanting plants*<br>• *Applying the concept of companion planting in gardening* | • Box: approx. 25cm deep x 50cm wide x 30cm high<br>• 5 small vegetable or flowered plants. Bear in mind that plants will need space to grow<br>• Potting soil<br>• Plastic cups, 1 per child<br>• Spray bottles or plastic bottles from Unit 2, Lesson 1<br>• Materials to decorate the box with paint or markers. Use light-colored paints for hot climates.<br>• The Vegetable Plot CD, *Little Green Heads*, track 5<br>• Optional- plastic insects to prepare for next lesson | W • Little Green Heads p. 15<br>O • Little Green Heads p. 20<br>I • Garden in the Box p. 9<br>• Plant Me pp. 10-11 |
| **Technology**<br>**All Ages**<br>• Use the *Our Planting Chart* poster to document the name of the plant, a drawing and the month it was planted<br>**5yrs+**<br>• Observation and documentation of the growth of the *Garden in the Box* or garden with a camera or picture-taking device | • *Developing observation skills*<br>• *Extending documentation techniques* | • Camera or picture-taking device<br>• Voice-recording device | • *Our Planting Chart* class poster |

## Guiding Questions

**Our Green Question**
*Why are we growing our vegetables in a box?*

## Before and During the Lesson

- Do you remember what plants need to grow?
- Can you remember which plants are friends?
- How can we plan our garden using drawings?

## End of Lesson Reflection

- What did we plant?
- What do we need to do when we plant a seed?
- When will our fruit and vegetables be ready to eat?

## Teacher Set-up

- Plan on 1-2 hours preparation time plus the outing to your local nursery to select the plants.
- Have enough plants, one for every child plus a few extras, in case a plant is destroyed. This can easily happen especially with young children.
- Select 5-6 plants from the quick-maturing small fruit and vegetable plants described below for your *Garden in the Box*. These can be eaten raw and have relatively shallow roots.
    - o Show children colorful edible flowers such as pansies, marigolds or chives (check seasonality).
    - o Use small fast-growing herbs and leafy lettuces.
    - o Use strawberries plants that are already beginning to flower (check seasonality).
    - o Use a variety of vegetables: small root (baby carrots or radishes), stalk (fennel), leafy (Brazilian spinach) and/or bulb vegetables (spring onions).
    - o For a tactile exploration, use plants with soft hairy leaves such as sage or lambs-ear that tickle when touched.
    - o To combine hearing, movement, and texture, include grasses as they stimulate all three senses and make noise when different grasses are planted together.
- Refer to the chart on the next page to assess how long each plant will take to mature in order to plan the duration of the *Garden in the Box*. Complete the charts on pages 90-92 with the plants you have selected and why.
- If using a wooden crate, line each box with plastic film on the inside, and puncture some holes or slits in the bottom. If using a plastic tub or box, drill some holes at the bottom to allow for drainage. Plan on preparing one box for every 4 to 5 children. This gives each child the opportunity to work in a group without being too cramped! If this is not possible, try to prepare boxes for as many smaller groups as you can.
- Fill the box halfway with compost soil for the children. Add some seeds or other treasures to the box of soil. You can even add plastic insects or earthworms to introduce the next lesson on friends of the garden. Place a large container with the rest of the soil in the center of the room.

**Teacher's Tips**
If planting on a plot of land, getting the right consistency of soil is key. Here is a recipe for good compost: look at the color, it should be dark, light, soft, and permeable. Mix it with a bit of thin gravel and a bit of manure. If the earth is "clayey" add some red soil. If the soil is too pale and sandy, add some compost.

# > Seasonal Chart

Example of seasonality in the tropics around the Equator. The ticks show the best time to plant.

| CROP NAME | MATURITY | JAN | FEB | MAR | APR | MAY | JUN | JUL | AUG | SEP | OCT | NOV | DEC |
|---|---|---|---|---|---|---|---|---|---|---|---|---|---|
|  beets | 40-70 days | | | | ✓ | ✓ | ✓ | | | | | | |
| black beans  | 60 days | ✓ | ✓ | ✓ | | | | | | ✓ | ✓ | ✓ | |
|  tomatoes | 60-150 days | | ✓ | ✓ | ✓ | ✓ | | | | | | | |
| spinach  | 70-90 days | ✓ | ✓ | | | | | | | ✓ | ✓ | ✓ | ✓ |
|  onions | 50-120 days | | ✓ | ✓ | ✓ | ✓ | ✓ | ✓ | ✓ | ✓ | ✓ | ✓ | |
| carrots  | 90 days | | | ✓ | ✓ | ✓ | ✓ | | | | | | |
|  radishes | 30-50 days | ✓ | ✓ | ✓ | ✓ | ✓ | ✓ | ✓ | ✓ | ✓ | ✓ | ✓ | ✓ |
| coriander  | 60-90 days | ✓ | ✓ | ✓ | ✓ | ✓ | | | ✓ | ✓ | ✓ | ✓ | ✓ |

## Project Chart 1 Time frame ............................................................

| Plant name | Season | Type (fruit/veg/herb) | Fruit/Veg color group (green, blue/purple, red, yellow/orange, brown/white) | Days to mature | Key characteristics |
|---|---|---|---|---|---|
| | | | | | |
| | | | | | |
| | | | | | |
| | | | | | |
| | | | | | |
| | | | | | |
| | | | | | |
| | | | | | |
| | | | | | |
| | | | | | |
| | | | | | |
| | | | | | |
| | | | | | |
| | | | | | |
| | | | | | |

## Project Chart 2

Time frame ..............................................................

| Plant name | Season | Type (fruit/veg/herb) | Fruit/Veg color group (green, blue/purple, red, yellow/orange, brown/white) | Days to mature | Key characteristics |
|---|---|---|---|---|---|
| | | | | | |
| | | | | | |
| | | | | | |
| | | | | | |
| | | | | | |
| | | | | | |
| | | | | | |
| | | | | | |
| | | | | | |
| | | | | | |
| | | | | | |
| | | | | | |
| | | | | | |
| | | | | | |
| | | | | | |

## Project Chart 3

Time frame ..........................................................................

| Plant name | Season | Type (fruit/veg/herb) | Fruit/Veg color group (green, blue/purple, red, yellow/orange, brown/white) | Days to mature | Key characteristics |
|---|---|---|---|---|---|
| | | | | | |
| | | | | | |
| | | | | | |
| | | | | | |
| | | | | | |
| | | | | | |
| | | | | | |
| | | | | | |
| | | | | | |
| | | | | | |
| | | | | | |
| | | | | | |
| | | | | | |
| | | | | | |
| | | | | | |

## Arts

*How can we plan our Garden in the Box?*

**5yrs+**

- The beauty of planting and growing is that it also develops children's planning skills, as they have to think ahead and plan for seasonality and space. This is an excellent opportunity to get children to **design** their **plot of land** and/or the layout of the plants in their ***Garden in the Box*** or garden.

- Place children in groups of four or five (if possible, or else as many smaller groups as you can) and hand out a **piece of card** or the **plot template** on page 95. Ask the children to think about companion plants and which combinations work well together. Ask them to **design** their own vegetable plot by **drawing** the plants in each square, first with pencil and then a **black marker**, finally **coloring** them in with ink or markers.

## Science & Nature

*What are the important things to remember when planting a Garden in the Box?*

**All Ages**

- If possible, put children into groups of 4 or 5 per box. Ask them to **look** for their little treasures as they **dig** their fingers through the **soil**. This will give children the incentive to get their hands dirty and **manipulate the soil** (not all children are comfortable getting their hands "dirty" with soil).

- Once children have had ample time to play with the soil, ask them to **fill** the rest of the **box** with the **potting soil**, 2cm from the brim (top) of the box. Children can use **plastic cups** to transport the soil from the bag to the box. Take the first plant out of its pot, **showing the roots** and how delicate they are, explaining that plants must **keep their roots intact**. Stress the importance of **planting** it at exactly the **right depth**, not too deep (danger of rotting) nor too shallow (drying out the roots). Let children take turns, one by one, as you ensure that every step is done correctly. Once all the plants have been planted, **place** the *Garden in the Box* in a **sunny spot**, that isn't too warm.

- **Complete** the *Garden in the Box Chart* on page 96 with the plants you have used for the project for your own records.

Before doing the journal activities, **play** and **dance** along with the song *Little Green Heads*, from The Vegetable Patch CD (track 5).

Ask children to **stick a seed** in the middle of the hand on *Little Green Heads*, page 15 of their journal, to remind them that every plant starts from a seed.

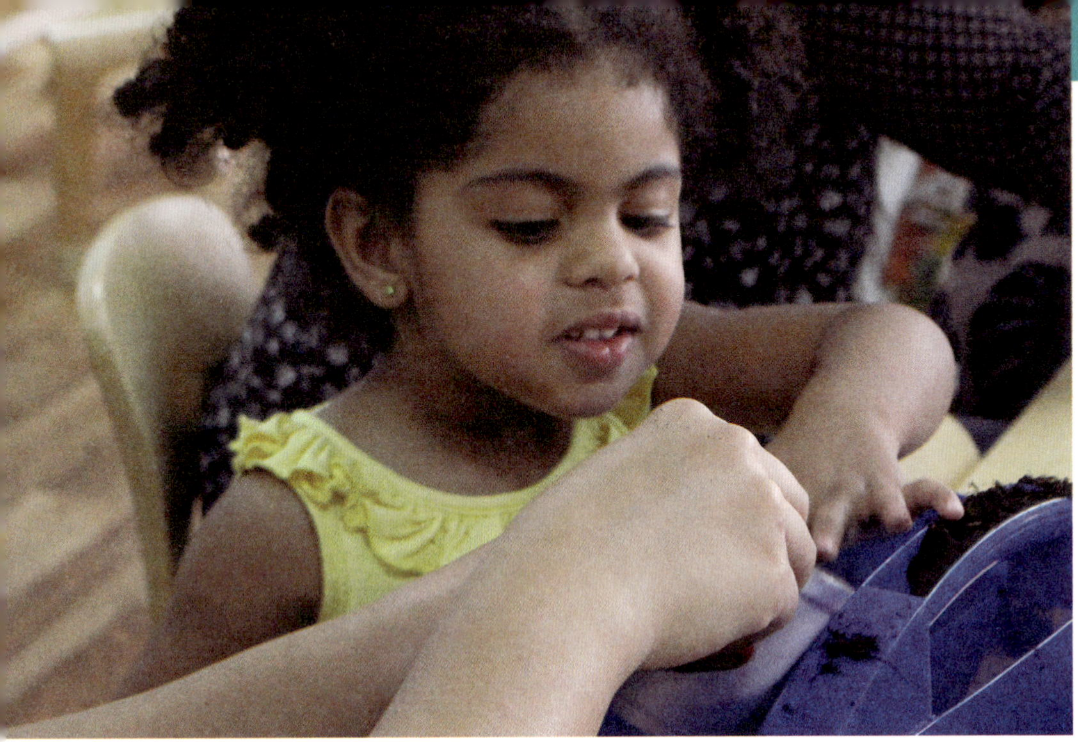

0 Ask children to **draw** a little **sprout** growing from the ground on *Little Green Heads*, page 20 of their journal, to remind them that it takes a lot of patience to wait for a seedling to grow into a plant.

1 Ask children to **document** their *Garden in the Box* or garden by **taking a picture** of it and adding it to their journal on the *Garden in the Box* activity on page 9 of their journal. Next, have the students **record** the fruit and vegetables they are planting by **coloring** the **squares** in the color of that given month on the *Plant Me* chart on pages 10 and 11.

## Technology

*How can we use technology to see our garden grow?*

### All Ages

- Complete the *Our Planting Chart* class poster together, to record the name of the plant, a drawing of it, and the month it was planted.

### 5yrs+

- Document the growth of your *Garden in the Box* or outside garden with a camera or picture-taking device that allows you to time-lapse your project. Consider also documenting the changes through voice recording.

### Teacher's Tips

- Show children pictures of how the plants will look once they grow. Alternatively, you may want to keep this a surprise.
- Organize and delegate responsibility for caring for the plants.

## Garden in the Box Chart

| picture | picture | picture | picture | picture |
|---|---|---|---|---|
| | | | | |
| Plant name | Plant name | Plant name | Plant name | Plant name |

## Observations

# Friends of The Garden

*Finding out who are the wanted or unwanted guests of our garden!*

This lesson focuses on identifying those creatures that are vitally important to the health of our garden as well as identifying those that are considered "pests" and unwanted guests. For example, bees are our biggest friends and helpers! It's been estimated that one third of all our food supply relies on bees and the role they play in pollinating plants. Whether they're gathering nectar or specifically gathering pollen, they are essential for allowing plants to develop fruit and vegetables. They are vitally important to crops around the world and to some of the plants you will grow (fruit and vegetables mainly in the spring and summer months).

Help children understand that a gentle equilibrium exists in nature and we can play a role to facilitate it. Balance and respect are the key words.

Science & Nature

Arts

Math

**Wonder**
- Friend or Pest? Friend! p. 16
- Friends or Pests? Pests! p. 17
- Friends of the Garden pp. 18-19

**Observation**
- Busy Bees p. 21
- Friends of the Garden p. 22

**Investigation**
- Ladybug Spots p. 12

**Vocabulary**
bees, ladybugs, earthworms, aphids, slugs/snails, caterpillars, friends, pests, sap, spots, stripes, long, thick, round, small

*Artie's Community Garden,* (track 10)

| ACTIVITY | SKILLS | MATERIALS | JOURNALS |
|---|---|---|---|
| **Science & Nature**<br>**All Ages**<br>• Garden hunt to find creatures in the garden | • *Identifying garden friends*<br>• *Identifying garden pests* | • Pictures of bees, ladybugs, slugs/ snails, caterpillars and earthworms<br>• Magnifying glasses to observe the bugs you find from close up<br>• Bees and ladybugs cut-outs (3yrs+)<br>• Scissors<br>• Glue<br>• Brown crayons<br>• The Vegetable Plot CD, *Artie's Community Garden*, track 10 | W • Friend or Pest? Friend! p. 16<br>• Friends or Pests? Pests! p. 17<br>• Friends of the Garden pp. 18-19<br>O • Busy Bees p. 21 |
| **Arts**<br>**4yrs+**<br>• Pattern completion of ladybugs and bees, inspired by Aboriginal drawings | • *Identifying storytelling cues through images and Aboriginal art*<br>• *Identifying patterns*<br>• *Reproducing patterns* | **4-5yrs**<br>• Scissors<br>• Glue<br>• Bees and ladybugs cut-outs | O • Friends of the Garden p. 22 |
| **Math**<br>**5yrs+**<br>• Understanding the concept of odd and even by counting the number of spots on a ladybug | • *Identifying and using symmetry to find even numbers*<br>• *Categorizing a number as odd or even depending on the number of spots on the ladybug's wing covers (elytra)* | • Black and colored pencils | I • Ladybug Spots p. 12 |

## Guiding Questions

**Our Green Question**
*Why is it important for our garden to have friends (but not pests)?*

## Before and During the Lesson

- Can you name some creatures you can find in the garden?
- Can you see any creatures? Can you identify or see their eyes/legs/wings?
- Are the creatures friends or pests of the garden?

## End of Lesson Reflection

- What does a ladybug/bee/earthworm/aphid/slug/snail/caterpillar look like?
- What friend of the garden eats a pest of the garden?
- How can you help keep pests of the garden away, without harming them?

**Teacher Set-Up**

- If you are unable to go on a nature hunt you can prepare pictures of bees, ladybugs, slugs/snails, caterpillars, and earthworms and place them in your Garden in the Box. Have some magnifying glasses handy to start observing friends and pests of the garden.

## Science & Nature

*Who are the friends and pests of the garden?*

### All Ages

- If you **look closely** enough you will find that your garden is **full of creatures**, some are helpful and others less so. Go on a "*friends and pests of the garden*" hunt. If an outing isn't possible, use pictures instead.

- Talk about ***friends*** of the garden:

    - ***Bees***: Bees are extremely important for gardeners because they take a powder called pollen from flower to flower. This is called pollination, and it makes plants grow new fruit, vegetables, and seeds. Growing flowers that bees like will help your plants to grow better. Bees are friends of the garden, but we must not touch them as they can sting us.

    - ***Ladybugs***: Ladybugs like to feed off the aphids that are on some plants, which is why gardeners think it's a sign of good luck to see one in their garden.

    - ***Earthworms***: Earthworms feed on soil, plant remains, and dead insects. They pull the leaves into the soil and they dig up the soil, increasing soil fertility.

- Talk about ***pests***, unwanted guests of the garden:

    - ***Slugs and snails***: Slugs and snails love to munch their way through plants with juicy leaves, such as lettuce. Every time you see a slug or snail on or near your plants, pick them off and put them in an open area of your garden.

    - ***Caterpillars***: Caterpillars feed on the leaves and flowers of many plants. Look for holes in the middle or around the edges of leaves and petals. If you find caterpillars on young plants, pick them off and take them away from your garden.

    - ***Aphids and whiteflies***: Aphids and whiteflies are tiny insects that swarm onto leaves and stems of some plants. They suck out sap – the liquid inside a plant – and keep the plant from growing properly. Gently wipe off any aphids you see using a sheet of paper towel.

- If you find any **small insects**, use the **magnifying glasses** and ask the children to **observe** the creatures up-close, if possible. Children **identify friends or pests** of the garden. Ask them to look for the eyes, legs, wings (if any).

Play the song *Artie's Community Garden*, on The Vegetable Patch CD (track 10). The song deals with how people can eat vegetables and still be friends of the garden – it's about balance.

**Teacher's Tips**
To keep slugs and snails away from your plants (if you have planted outdoors) put some cracked eggshells around your plants. Slugs and snails need a smooth surface to move around so the eggshells will keep them away from your plants.

W — Complete the three *Friend or Pest?* activities on pages 16-19 of the journal with findings.

O — Flowers attract bees and other pollinators that are needed for our plants to grow fruit and vegetables. Finish the *Busy Bees* flower garden on page 21 of the journal, making sure to paint lots of bees buzzing around!

## Arts

*How can we tell a story about insects using images and symbols?*

**4yrs+**

- **Australian Aboriginal art** uses **symbols** to tell the story of Aboriginal history and culture. It uses a set of basic elements such as dots, curved and straight lines and concentric circles. Normally concentric circles represent campsites, straight lines represent routes or paths and circles represent camps or other places of interest. Wavy lines usually represent water in some form.

O — Inspired by Australian Aboriginal art, complete the insects' circular journeys with ladybugs and bee cut-outs on the *Friends of the Garden* activity on page 22 of the journal.

## Math

*How can we tell whether the number of spots on a ladybug is odd or even?*

**5yrs+**

- A ladybug is an insect that has six legs, a head, two antennae, two eyes, two wings and two wing covers called "elytra". At birth the ladybug's elytra are soft and yellow but as the ladybug grows older, its color darkens.

- A ladybug can have different number of spots on its elytra. When equal number of spots can be seen on either side of its elytra, they are said to be *symmetrical* and the number of spots is even. When there is one spot in the middle of the two elytra, making the spots *asymmetrical* then the number of spots is odd.

Turn to *Ladybug Spots* on page 12 of your journal and complete the ladybugs, one with an even and the other with an odd number of spots on its elytra. Not all ladybugs are red with black dots, so you can be creative with the colors you use!

## Observations

## Unit 3
# Growing

Sowing and growing are exciting for children. They motivate learning, develop self-confidence and encourage collaboration, helping to support personal, social and emotional objectives. In addition, they bring young children into meaningful contact with the diversity of nature.

This unit will focus on the skills needed to care for plants (for example - watering) and the observational skills that develop as the children learn to see the differences in plants as they watch them grow.

**In this Unit:**

- Lesson 1: Caring for Plants: Watering and Water's Properties
- Lesson 2: Observing and Documenting a Life Cycle
- Lesson 3: Discovering Fruit & Vegetable Shapes
- Lesson 4: Watch the Plants Grow

**Unit Goals**

- Caring for potted plants through watering
- Careful observation and documentation of changes in plants and the life cycle of a seed
- Developing early math skills through measuring, classification, and shape recognition

# Caring for Plants: Watering and Water's Properties

*Develop hand-eye coordination and measuring skills through caring for plants.*

Children explore the connections between water and living things, delighting in water's value as a resource and its varied nature. By the end of this lesson, children will master watering a plant and learn how to care for their Garden in the Box for the weeks to come. In addition, they will explore ways in which they can measure the temperature of water by crafting their own thermometers.

This activity teaches children responsibility for living things while practicing math and measuring concepts.

Science & Nature

Engineering

**Wonder**
- Rain, Rain, Come Again! p. 20

**Observation**
- Let It Rain! p. 23

**Investigation**
- Investigating Temperature p. 13

**Vocabulary**
water, rain, thirsty, watering can, hot, cold, pour, wet, dry, spill, fill, sprinkle, measure, temperature, thermometer.
Quantifiers: a little bit, a lot of, just right

**5yrs+**
*The Rain Song,*
(track 3)

| ACTIVITY | SKILLS | MATERIALS | JOURNALS |
|---|---|---|---|
| **Engineering**<br>**All Ages**<br>• Creation of a thermometer using a piece of card, the template and elastic<br>• Identification of hot and cold water temperatures | • *Identifying and finding ways to measure water temperature*<br>• *Investigating the difference between water temperatures using the card thermometer* | • The Vegetable Plot CD *The Rain Song*, track 3<br>• Thermometer template<br>• Rectangular strip of card, 7 x 15cm, with perforated holes at approx. 3.5cm from either end of the strip. Prepare one per child for children aged 3 to 4yrs old<br>• Glue<br>• White elastic cord<br>• Red and blue markers<br>• Water<br>• 2 washing up bowls (one for warm and the other for cold water)<br>• Dry soil in a pot or bowl | I • Investigating Temperature p. 13 |
| **Science & Nature**<br>**All Ages**<br>• Demonstration of how to water plants in the Garden in the Box and/or garden<br>• Shared responsibility for watering plants<br>**Project Ideas**<br>• Predicting of how much water plants will need by observing nature's clues | • *Developing hand-eye coordination to successfully pour water*<br>• *Observing nature's clues to help us know our plants' needs* | • Small watering can<br>OR<br>• Plastic bottles or cups (from Unit 1, Lesson 4)<br>• Plant pot or plastic cup for transplanting/potting<br>• Printed Water Chart from page 111<br>• Blue paint (1 or more shade of blue)<br>• Cotton buds (3 yrs)<br>• One or more pine cones | W • Rain, Rain, Come Again! p. 20<br>O • Let It Rain! p. 23 |

## Guiding Questions

**Our Green Question**
*Why is it important to water our plants properly?*

## Before and During the Lesson

- Why do plants need water?
- How do plants like to be watered? (stems/soil/leaves)
- How often do we need to water our plants?

## End of Lesson Reflection

- How can you tell a plant needs water?
- What water temperature is best to water the plants?
- How can we record when we water our plants?

## Teacher Set-Up

- For children aged 3 to 4, prepare one card thermometer for each child before starting the activity.
- **Create a card thermometer** by cutting a **strip of card**, 7 cm by 15 cm, and gluing the **thermometer template** on top. **Puncture holes** at each end of the card. Cut a piece of your white elastic cord. Color half of the elastic cord red and the other half blue with your markers. Next, thread it through both the holes and tie a knot at the back of the thermometer so that the elastic cord can slide up and down.

## Engineering

*How can we measure water temperature without touching it? What colors do we use to show hot and cold?*

### All Ages

Begin the class by **talking about water and rain** and the fact that plants need water to live and grow. Play **The Rain Song** from The Vegetable Plot CD (track 3). See if the children remember the chorus. Have them make rain sounds and movements with their fingers and hands as they sing along. *How do plants get water when there is no rain?* Explain that when we care for plants indoors or when there is no rain outdoors, we have to water plants ourselves.

- Group children into smaller groups and prepare two **washing up bowls** of water per group (or table) – one with warm water (make sure it's not too hot) and the other with cold. Ask them to talk about how the different temperatures of water feel on their hands and lead the discussion to the fact that plants don't like cold water or hot water but water that is at **room temperature** (just right).

- Explain to children that we can measure the temperature of water without touching it by using a thermometer. Have your **hand-made thermometer** available. **Demonstrate** the way you can **move** the **elastic up or down** depending on how the ***temperature*** feels. If it's hot, make the red line longer, if it's cold, pull the elastic in the opposite direction to make the blue line longer.

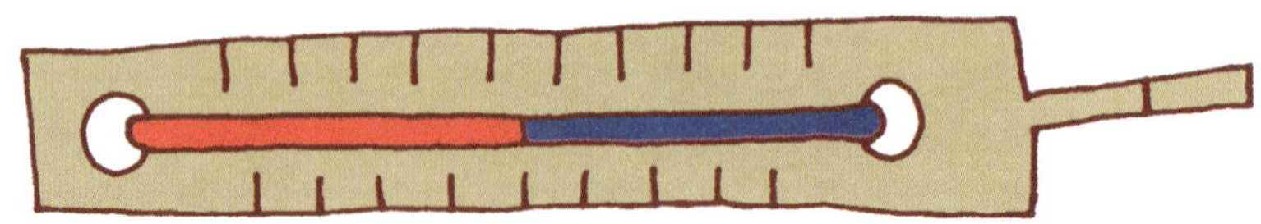

- Now ask children to **make their own thermometers** and hand out the rectangular pieces of card, thermometer templates, and pieces of white elastic. Ask children to color half of the elastic red and the other half blue. Next, they loop the elastic through the perforated holes. Help them to tie the two ends together at the back. Children aged 3-4 can practice on ready-made thermometers.
- Ask the children to **show you what cold, hot, and lukewarm** room temperature water **looks like** on their thermometers.

I

Children find their ideal water temperature by coloring their thermometer red from the top down to the middle and blue from the middle down to the bottom, to find the temperature in the middle that's 'just right' in the *Investigating Temperatures* activity on page 13 of their journal.

## Science & Nature

*How often do we need to water our plants?*
*How do we know when a plant needs water?*

### All Ages

- Now **show** them how to water plants. Fill the watering can with water, pointing out that it is heavier now because it is filled with water. Demonstrate watering by **slowly watering the base of the plant**, directly onto the soil, without wetting the leaves.

- Now let the **children try**, making sure they pour the water slowly, not spilling water out of the box. Water until all the soil is wet, remembering that plants don't like to have "wet feet", which happens when we give plants too much water.
- Allow children to **compare a separate pot of dry soil** to show them that if it's dry, they need to water the plant and soil. **After 1 or 2 days** (or whenever the soil is dry) ask the children to feel the soil again with their fingers and if it's dry then make sure to **water the plants again**.
- **Distribute the responsibility for caring for** and watering for the **Garden in the Box** throughout the class. Tasks include:
    - Feeling the soil to see how dry or wet it is
    - Checking the water temperature
    - Filling the bottle or watering can with water
    - Watering the Garden in the Box
    - Documenting the amount of water that has been poured with drops of water on the Water Chart.

**Document water amounts** on the **Water Chart** on page 111 (one drop of water or blue mark indicates small quantities of water used versus two or three drops for more). **Rotate the tasks** between all the children so that every child has the chance to perform each task and at least one task more than once.

W

Remind children how important rain is for their plants. Guide the children into making rain sounds with their fingers. Demonstrate tapping one finger on your palm, next two fingers as the rain gets heavier, then four, five, and finally clap for heavy rain. Now add the visual component by asking them to print rain coming down from the clouds using blue paint and cotton buds on the *Rain, Rain, Come Again!* activity on page 20 of their journals.

O

Plants can't talk to tell you that they are thirsty but they can give you signs that they are lacking water. **Point out visual cues**, like drooping or yellow leaves, that indicate when a plant is thirsty and ask children to identify which of the two plants on their journal needs water. Ask them to **finger paint rain** from the clouds to give them water on the *Let it Rain* activity on page 23 of their journal.

**Teacher's Tips**

Each plant has different needs, so check the water needs for each plant before you start this activity. For example, humidity on the leaves can cause fungal infections in some plants, but plants from tropical, humid places love being sprayed with mist. Outdoor gardens don't have a problem with excess water, as the water will penetrate deeper in the soil and leave the plants unharmed.

## Project Ideas

### All Ages

- **Set up a weather station** in your classroom by using one or more **pine cones**. Pine cones open and close depending on how much water is in the air. If the air is humid and it is going to rain, they close and if the air is dry, they open up. Ask the children to observe the pine cones to decide whether or not their plants are going to need extra water.

## Observations

# > Water Chart

Week beginning: ..............................................................................................

| DAY | NAME | AMOUNT OF WATER [BY DROPS] |
|---|---|---|
| Monday | | A LITTLE / SOME / A LOT |
| Tuesday | | A LITTLE / SOME / A LOT |
| Wednesday | | A LITTLE / SOME / A LOT |
| Thursday | | A LITTLE / SOME / A LOT |
| Friday | | A LITTLE / SOME / A LOT |

# Observing and Documenting a Life Cycle

*Learn to sprout a seed and observe the life cycle of a living organism.*

This activity provides children with a wealth of experience, introducing them to the surprises of the plant world, to develop their curiosity and desire to investigate. They will look for changes from seed to plant and, as budding scientists, will record the changes on the Life Cycle pages of their journals.

Science & Nature

**Wonder**
- Sprouting a Seed p. 21

**Observation**
- Observing a Life Cycle p. 24

**Investigation**
- Life Cycle Journal pp. 14-15

**Vocabulary**
the names of bean seeds available in your area, grow, seed, soil, leaf, leaves, stem, big, small, sprout

*Little Green Heads,*
(track 5)

| ACTIVITY | SKILLS | MATERIALS | JOURNALS |
|---|---|---|---|
| **Science & Nature**<br>**All Ages**<br>• Sow a seed in a cup of soil to sprout a seed<br>• Observation and documentation of the stages of a sprout in the journal<br>• Transplanting the healthiest baby plants into the Garden in the Box | • *Developing observational skills to notice the changes a sprout goes through*<br>• *Developing fine motor skills by sowing a seed in soil*<br>• *Documenting the stages of a sprout* | • One transparent plastic cup, or reused plastic bottle cut in half, per child<br>• One large seed to sow per child/small group. For example, fava (broad) bean or sunflowers in the summer. Radish seeds can be used if you need ones that sprout quickly<br>• Soil<br>• Spray bottle<br>• The Vegetable Plot CD *Little Green Heads*, track 5<br>• Garden in the Box | W • Sprouting a Seed p. 21<br>O • Observing a Life Cycle p. 24<br>I • Life Cycle Journal pp. 14-15 |

## Guiding Questions

**Our Green Question**
*Why does a sprout get bigger?*

## Before and During the Lesson

- Do you think all our seeds will grow?
- Is it important how deep you plant a seed?
- How many roots and leaves can you see? (after 15 days)

## End of Lesson Reflection

- Are the sprouting plants the same or are they different?
- What stages did you observe of the life cycle?
- How can we help our plants grow?

## Teacher Set-up

- You will need to allow ample time, normally at least 15 days, for seeds to sprout so that the children can observe the different stages of the life cycle. If you need a faster-growing seed, radishes sprout more quickly. Make sure to check how long the seeds you have chosen need to germinate and plan accordingly.

- You may want to plant a few extra seeds in case some don't grow. This is an opportunity for children to learn about the unpredictability of nature.

## Science & Nature

*What happens when we plant a seed? Can you see the seed under the soil?*

### All Ages

Play the **Little Green Heads** (track 5) song and ask the children to do the actions to review how we plant a seed.

- This lesson will review **seeds** and explain their importance at the beginning of a new plant's life. Hold your seed up and show it to the children and ask them what it is. Large bean seeds like fava (broad) beans are best for this activity. Encourage the children to talk about what the seed looks and feels like.

- Give every child a **transparent plastic cup** or reuse the bottom half of an old plastic water bottle (make sure there are no sharp edges). Demonstrate how to **fill the cup with soil** 1cm to the **brim**. **Distribute two seeds** per child and ask them to **press** the **seed** approximately 0.5cm into the **soil (pat it down)**, making sure that they are not both in the same spot and not visible to the eye.

- *How can we help our plants to grow?* Talk about how a baby plant gets its food (or nutrients) from the soil through its roots and leaves. It's important to give plants water and sunlight to help them grow.

- **Spray the soil** with your spray bottle and keep the soil moist for the following days and place by a sunny window until the seeds germinate. Continue to water.

W: Highlight that most sprouts go through **four stages of a life cycle** and ask children to **observe** the sprouts after 6-10 days and 11-15 days, recording the differences on the *Sprouting a Seed* activity on page 21.

O: Ask the children to **observe** how many **small leaves** they can see on their sprouting seed and to **complete** the little sprout on the *Observing a Life Cycle* activity on page 24.

I: Ask the children to record the **changes** to their **sprouting seeds** in the *Life Cycle Journal* on pages 14-15.

## Science & Nature

*Did all the seeds sprout? Whose seeds sprouted first? Are all the sprouting plants the same or are they different? How can we choose which baby plants to transplant into our Garden in the Box?*

### All Ages

- After the seeds have sprouted, select three or four of the healthiest looking plants and ask the children to transplant the baby plants into your Garden in the Box or garden. Ask them to dig a little hole in the soil. Take the plant out of the cup by turning the cup upside down and gently wiggling the seedling out. Ask them to firm the plant in the Garden in the Box or garden, making sure that it has enough space to grow into a bigger plant.

## Observations

1–5 days

6–10 days

11–15 days

16–20 days

# Discovering Fruit & Vegetable Shapes

*Shape recognition using plants, fruit, and vegetables.*

The most obvious changes children notice in plant growth are in size, shape, and color. In this lesson, we will introduce shapes and colors related to fruit, vegetables, and plants whilst activating their taste buds! Children are more readily engaged when they can relate the material to real life contexts.

It's important that children learn to define themselves through their own likes and dislikes from first-hand experiences. Before a child can say they like or dislike a fruit or vegetable, make sure they have had a chance to taste it (being mindful of food allergies). They might just be surprised about how tasty a fruit or veggie can actually be!

**Math** **Arts** **Science & Nature**

**W** **Wonder**
- Foodscape pp. 22-23
- Sensory Page p. 28

**O** **Observation**
- Triangles and Circles and Squares... Oh My! p. 25
- Sensory Page p. 32

**I** **Investigation**
- X-Ray Onions p. 16
- Sensory Page p. 31

**Vocabulary**
circle, square, apple, sweet, sour, red, yellow, green, long, leaves, vegetables, apple, lettuce, onion, Do you like...? Yes I do, No, I don't

| ACTIVITY | SKILLS | MATERIALS | JOURNALS |
|---|---|---|---|
| **Math**<br>**All Ages**<br>• Introduction and revision of shapes: circle, square, and triangle<br>• Use of fruit and vegetables to identify shapes | • *Developing early math skills through shape and color recognition*<br>• *Learning to classify shapes* | • Circle and Square flashcards<br>• Apples, pears, oranges, lettuce, onions, broccoli, cauliflower, and other fruit and vegetables | O • Triangles and Circles and Squares… Oh My! p. 25 |
| **Arts**<br>**3-4yrs**<br>• Creation of a foodscape with fruit and vegetable prints<br>**5yrs+**<br>• Use halved onions to make an "X-ray" image of the onion and count its layers | • *Developing fine motor skills*<br>• *Expanding compositional skills with the use of print-making techniques*<br>• *Contrasting black/white* | **3-4yrs**<br>• Variety of halved fruit and vegetables, for example, celery stalks, onions, broccoli, cauliflower<br>• Poster paint: green, yellow, red, blue, brown<br>• Plastic plate for poster paint<br>**5yrs+**<br>• Black card<br>• Onions, cut horizontally and vertically<br>• White poster paint<br>• Plastic plate for poster paint | W • Foodscape pp. 22-23<br>I • X-Ray Onions p. 16 |
| **Science & Nature**<br>**Project Ideas**<br>**All Ages**<br>• Categorization of food tastes using different flavored mangoes | • *Identifying flavors and associating the flavors with different mangoes* | • Variety of mangos with distinctly different tastes cut into small slices. | W • Sensory Page p. 28<br>O • Sensory Page p. 32<br>I • Sensory Page p. 31 |

## Guiding Questions

**Our Green Question**
*What shapes can we see in fruit and vegetables?*

## Before and During the Lessone

- What shapes can we see around us?
- What shapes are fruit and vegetables?
- Do fruit and vegetables change shape when you cut them in half?

## End of Lesson Reflection

- What are the most common shapes found in vegetables? What about fruit?
- Do you like ____________________? (name of fruit/vegetable)
- Do fruits and vegetables taste the same? What's different?

### Teacher Set-Up

Prepare a selection of fruit and vegetables of different colors and shapes. You can use fruit and vegetables that are ready from the Garden in the Box or garden. Leave some of these whole to display as an example and cut the rest in half, cutting some vertically and some horizontally.

### Math

*What happens if you cut fruit and vegetables in half?*
*Can you name some shapes?*
*What shape is a pepper/onion/okra/carrot?*

**All Ages**

- Use the **visuals of shapes** on page 125. Point to the circle. Outline with your finger demonstrating making a circle shape. Ask the children what shape it is. Now point to the **square** visual, and count each of the four sides, counting *one, two, three, four*. Encourage children to point to other square-shaped objects in the room.

- **Say** the **chant** and ask the children to make **circular motions** when describing the **circle** and **square** motions when describing the square.

**Circle + Square Rhyme**

This is a circle, 'round and 'round.
(make circular motions)
This is a circle that I found.

There is a square with four sides the same
(make square motions).
This is a square, that's my name.

- Show the **basket** with whole and halved (horizontally and vertically) **fruit and vegetables**. Ask the children to observe the shapes that we can see in the fruit and vegetables. For example, small peppers are round, like circles, and carrots look like triangles. After that, explore how the shapes change depending on how the fruit and vegetables are cut. Notice how most vegetables have a circular shape if cut horizontally.

Turn to the *Triangles and Circles and Squares... Oh My!* activity on page 25 of the journal and ask them **to observe and identify the shapes** on their page and modify them to become fruit and vegetables.

### Arts

*Which shapes can we see when we print with fruit and vegetables? Do all fruit and vegetable prints have the same shape?*

**All Ages**

- **Review** the **shapes** of the fruits and/or vegetables you are going to use.

- If the weather allows for it, use an outdoor space to do your print-making activity. Cut two onions in half two different ways, horizontally and vertically. **Apply paint** on the flat side of the surface. **Distribute the vegetables** and **practice** the **print-making** technique on black or colored card by placing the painted side of the vegetable on the card (a plastic fork can be stuck in the top of the onion to keep it from slipping out of the child's hand when printing)

- You can use **broccoli** for trees, the base of **celery stalks** for roses, a **lemon** for the sun, and **okra** for beautiful flower designs. For inspiration, look up **Bruno Munari's** print-making activities.

Explore the vegetable shapes children enjoyed the most by asking them to complete the *Foodscape* on pages 22-23 of the journal.

W O I Ask children to make a note of their answers on the *Sensory Page* at the end of their journals (Wonder p. 28, Observation p. 32, Investigation p. 31).

I X-ray your onions by dipping the onion in white paint and printing it on the black *X-ray Onion* activity on page 16 of the journal. Count the layers of the onion.

### Science & Nature

*Do all mangos taste the same? What flavors can you identify in mangos? What is your favorite flavor? Are the mangos__________________ (crunchy/soft/smooth/rough)?*

**All Ages**

- This activity provides the perfect opportunity to introduce flavors to children (make sure you've checked for food allergies before you ask the children to taste any of the fruit and vegetables you've selected). Select a variety of mangoes, ensuring that you have two contrasting flavors. Cut into thin slices and put in a bowl (one for each type of mango).

- Ask the children to taste the mangoes and to talk about flavors (sweet/sour/bitter/etc.), and which flavors they like or dislike. Give each child the opportunity to say *Yes, I do* or *No, I don't*. To extend the activity, you can ask questions about the textures of the food they've tasted.

triangle
rectangle
oval
square
circle

# Watch the Plants Grow

*Introduction to mathematical concepts of measurement through observation of plants.*

This activity should be repeated once or twice a week so that children can observe the changes taking place in their garden or Garden in the Box. The goal is for children to use language to describe mathematical concepts such as color, shape, size, and height.

Math

Technology

Arts

Science & Nature

**Observation**
- Observing Fruits in Nature p. 26

**Investigation**
- See How They Grow p. 17
- Measure Me! pp. 18-19
- Plant Growth Chart pp. 20-21

**Vocabulary**
How tall is...? How many leaves does...have? What shape is...? What color is...? taller than

*Squeeze Your Vegetables (The Growing Song),* (track 6)

| ACTIVITY | SKILLS | MATERIALS | JOURNALS |
| --- | --- | --- | --- |
| **Math**<br>**All Ages**<br>• Introduction of the concept and units of measurement<br>• Measurement of children (height)<br>**5yrs+**<br>• Measurement of one or two plants | • *Developing early numeracy skills*<br>• *Understanding the concept of measurement* | • Rulers, string, or blocks for younger children<br>• Pencils<br>• Large piece of paper to record children's heights<br>• The Vegetable Plot CD *Squeeze Your Vegetables (The Growing Song)*, track 6 | I • Measure Me! pp. 18-19 |
| **Science & Nature**<br>**All Ages**<br>• Documentation of plant growth on the classroom Growth Chart and journals (for children aged 5yrs and older)<br>**4yrs+**<br>• Observation of plant and fruit growth in nature | • *Observation of changes occurring in plants over time*<br>• *Documenting plant growth on a chart* | • Rulers, string, or blocks for younger children<br>• Pencils<br>• Classroom Growth Chart<br>• Images of the way local fruits grow in nature | O • Observing Fruits in Nature p. 26<br>I • Plant Growth Chart pp. 20-21 |
| **Technology**<br>**5yrs+**<br>• Documentation of growth with the use of a picture-taking device | • *Developing fine motor skills to hold a camera or phone*<br>• *Transforming black and white images into color* | • Picture-taking device (cell phone, camera, tablet) to take picture of the Garden in the Box<br>• Black and white photos of the garden/plant (one for each child/small group) | I • See How They Grow p. 17 |
| **Arts**<br>**Project Ideas**<br>**5yrs+**<br>• Children observe and draw the silhouettes of plants, interpreting the shadows | • *Exploring light and shadows to represent an image* | • Light (to make shadows)<br>• Paper<br>• Colored pencils/paints | |

## Guiding Questions

**Our Green Question**
*Why should we record our plants' growth?*

## Before and During the Lesson

- How tall are you? How can we measure our heights?
- How tall is the [name of plant]?
- How can we record how our plants are growing?

## End of Lesson Reflection

- Which plant grew the fastest?
- Does the sun/water affect how our plants grow?
- Why do we document the growth of our plants? What does it tell us?

## Math

How can we measure our plants to see that they are growing?

### All Ages

Use **whole-body movements** to convey the **concept of growth** by crouching down low and stretching up like a growing plant. Talk about how it relates to people too. Play track 6 **Squeeze Your Vegetables** (*The Growing Song* begins at 2:24) from The Vegetable Plot CD and dance around to the music, jumping or stretching up high every time you hear the word "*up*".

- Now introduce the concept of **measuring** as a way to **record** changes in **growth**. Line all the children up and **mark** their **heights** one by one on a large piece of paper that you've taped to the wall. Repeat this activity at the end of the project to see if there are any changes in the children's heights.

- Ask children what we can use to **measure things**. For children who haven't yet started to use measuring devices like a ruler, use blocks, stacking them one on top of the other as measurement tools. Let them **go around the room** and **measure objects** they find.

- Now take your Garden in the Box or go to your garden and **measure** the **plants** using a ruler or string.

Ask children to **draw one or two plants** on the *Measure Me!* activity on pages 18-19 of their journal. Children measure a plant one week, and then measure it again the following week, and then see how much it has grown.

## Science & Nature

*What can we learn from measuring our plants?*

### All Ages

- **Scientific investigation** involves the **act of collecting information** (capturing data) **over time** in order for it to help us better **understand** what we are investigating, in this case our plants. Measurements can also be a good indicator of the overall health of our plants.
- **Measure the plants** on a weekly basis for **4 weeks** using a ruler or string for older children or blocks for younger children.

Keep a **log** of **plant growth** on the classroom **Observation Charts** on pages 132-135.

O This is the perfect opportunity to observe the way fruits grow in nature. For example, bananas grow upside down from a bulb whereas pineapples grow upwards as a cluster of fruits. Ask children to complete the plants with their fruits on the *Observing Fruits in Nature* activity on page 26 of their journal.

I Ask children to document the **growth** of their plants on the *Plant Growth Chart* on pages 20-21 of their journal.

## Technology

*What devices can we use to observe changes in our plants?*

### 5yrs+

- Ask children take to **pictures** of the **Garden in the Box** or **garden** with a picture-taking device.
- Consider starting a 4-week **time-lapse project** of your garden. **Time-lapse** is a photographic technique in which a series of photos are taken at regular intervals over a long period of time. You can create time-lapse footage either by using this feature on your cell phone, or taking pictures of the Garden in the Box in the same position and then editing the images together in a video so that, when played at normal speed, things move faster and very slow changes become noticeable.

I **Print** a **black and white picture** of the garden for children to glue onto the *See How They Grow* activity on page 17 of their journals. They then transform these into color to represent their garden.

**Teacher's Tips**
Regularly observe and point out any differences in the way your plants have grown. Have some plants grown a lot faster than others? Did some of the plants get more sunlight than others? Does the amount of sun/water affect how our plants grow? This is a great activity for children to practice their linguistic skills thanks to its repetitive nature.

## Project Ideas

**Arts**

*What other techniques can you use to represent a life-size drawing of your plant?*

**5yrs+**

- You can extend the *Measure Me* activity in the journals by **casting a shadow of the plant** the child wants to draw in the journal by pointing a light above the plant and asking the child to draw the plant's silhouette. Children can later reinterpret the black and white shadows with colored pencils/paints.

## Observations

# > Observation Chart

Class ..........................................................................

| Day | Plant name | Plant height | Number of leaves | Leaf color | Flower color | Fruit or vegetable shape |
|---|---|---|---|---|---|---|
| Day 1 | | | | | | |
| Day 2 | | | | | | |
| Day 3 | | | | | | |
| Day 4 | | | | | | |
| Day 5 | | | | | | |
| Day 6 | | | | | | |
| Day 7 | | | | | | |
| Day 8 | | | | | | |
| Day 9 | | | | | | |
| Day 10 | | | | | | |
| Day 11 | | | | | | |
| Day 12 | | | | | | |
| Day 13 | | | | | | |
| Day 14 | | | | | | |
| Day 15 | | | | | | |

| Day | Plant name | Plant height | Number of leaves | Leaf color | Flower color | Fruit or vegetable shape |
|---|---|---|---|---|---|---|
| Day 16 | | | | | | |
| Day 17 | | | | | | |
| Day 18 | | | | | | |
| Day 19 | | | | | | |
| Day 20 | | | | | | |
| Day 21 | | | | | | |
| Day 22 | | | | | | |
| Day 23 | | | | | | |
| Day 24 | | | | | | |
| Day 25 | | | | | | |
| Day 26 | | | | | | |
| Day 27 | | | | | | |
| Day 28 | | | | | | |
| Day 29 | | | | | | |
| Day 30 | | | | | | |
| Day 31 | | | | | | |

# > Observation Chart

Class ..............................................................................

| Day | Plant name | Plant height | Number of leaves | Leaf color | Flower color | Fruit or vegetable shape |
|---|---|---|---|---|---|---|
| Day 1 | | | | | | |
| Day 2 | | | | | | |
| Day 3 | | | | | | |
| Day 4 | | | | | | |
| Day 5 | | | | | | |
| Day 6 | | | | | | |
| Day 7 | | | | | | |
| Day 8 | | | | | | |
| Day 9 | | | | | | |
| Day 10 | | | | | | |
| Day 11 | | | | | | |
| Day 12 | | | | | | |
| Day 13 | | | | | | |
| Day 14 | | | | | | |
| Day 15 | | | | | | |

| Day | Plant name | Plant height | Number of leaves | Leaf color | Flower color | Fruit or vegetable shape |
|---|---|---|---|---|---|---|
| Day 16 | | | | | | |
| Day 17 | | | | | | |
| Day 18 | | | | | | |
| Day 19 | | | | | | |
| Day 20 | | | | | | |
| Day 21 | | | | | | |
| Day 22 | | | | | | |
| Day 23 | | | | | | |
| Day 24 | | | | | | |
| Day 25 | | | | | | |
| Day 26 | | | | | | |
| Day 27 | | | | | | |
| Day 28 | | | | | | |
| Day 29 | | | | | | |
| Day 30 | | | | | | |
| Day 31 | | | | | | |

# Unit 4
# Harvesting

In this unit, children learn that there is a reason and a season for everything. At last, their patience will be rewarded and the fruit and vegetables they have tended to with so much care will come to maturity.

Children will delight in tasting the food they have grown, developing healthy eating habits!

**In this Unit:**

- Lesson 1: Vegetable Families
- Lesson 2: How Did Your Vegetables Grow?
- Lesson 3: Eating by Season
- Lesson 4: Eating the Rainbow

**Unit Goals**

- Learning about the seasonality of fruit and vegetables
- Categorizing vegetables by family type
- Collecting and counting fruit and vegetables
- Introducing and nurturing healthy eating habits by tasting a variety of fruit and vegetables

# Vegetable Families

*Counting vegetables and categorizing them by family type.*

Children learn to recognize and classify vegetables by family type, which is a skill that develops their counting abilities and math skills, in addition to using their creativity to make music with vegetables.

**Science & Nature** **Math** **Arts**

**Investigation**
- Vegetable Families pp. 22-23
- My Family Tree p. 24

**Vocabulary**
family, vegetables, bulb, flower, fruit, leaves, stem, seeds, onion, cauliflower, tomato, salad, peas, celery, potatoes, carrots or parsnips, numbers 1-10

*Mr. Potato,*
(track 8)

| ACTIVITY | SKILLS | MATERIALS | JOURNALS |
|---|---|---|---|
| **Science & Nature**<br>**All Ages**<br>• Introduction to the concept of vegetable family types<br><br>**5yrs+**<br>• Classification of vegetables into two or more family types | • *Developing classification skills of vegetables by family type* | • Images of vegetables<br>• Vegetable Families Chart<br>• The Vegetable Plot CD, *Mr Potato*, track 8 | J • Vegetable Families pp. 22-23 |
| **Math**<br>**All Ages**<br>• Identification and counting of vegetables<br>• Documentation of vegetables by family type<br><br>**5yrs+**<br>• Linking the concept of vegetable families with children's own family tree | • *Developing counting skills using vegetables* | • Garden in the Box<br>AND/OR<br>• Vegetables (one or more samples of each family type)<br>• Vegetable Families Chart | J • My Family Tree p. 24 |
| **Arts**<br>**All Ages**<br>• Creation of bell pepper instrument shakers using rice | • *Developing imagination by using vegetables in different ways (for example, to make instruments)*<br>• *Experimenting with high and low pitch sounds* | • Bell peppers (green, red and/or yellow), one per child<br>• Rice (uncooked)<br>• Other vegetables (for example, gourds)<br>• The Vegetable Plot CD, *Mr Potato*, track 8 | |

## Guiding Questions

**Our Green Question**
*Why do vegetables have family types?*

## Before and During the Lesson

- How do vegetables look different? How do they look the same?
- How can we group vegetables?
- Do you know vegetables have families like us?

## End of Lesson Reflection

- Can you remember the different vegetable families?
- What can we do to help us remember the different groups?
- Can you think of different ways to use vegetables?

## Science & Nature

*How can we group similar vegetables together? Can you remember the different family groups?*

### All Ages

- Ask children to think about their families and people in their family. Explain that vegetables have families just like us.

- There are two main ways to group vegetables, by the **edible part of the plant**, which is what we are using in this lesson, or by the **family relatedness**, which is closer to the way we group our own family (parents, children, grandparents, aunts, uncles, close and distant cousins, etc). By grouping our vegetables by the **part that we eat**, we are focusing children's attention on the edible qualities of the plant. *What are the most common parts of a vegetable we eat?* Ask the children to investigate and observe the vegetables at their local market. They will find that they are mainly **leaves** and **fruits**.

- Now talk about the **seven families** that all vegetables can be **categorized** into. Look for clues such as **where and how** the plants grow, such as root vegetables growing underground, or their **physical appearances**, for example, stem vegetables have long stems. You may want to only focus on some selected family groups depending on the age of the children.

  - Bulb (onion, garlic)
  - Flower (artichokes, cauliflower)
  - Fruit (tomato, zucchini)
  - Leaf (lettuce, spinach)
  - Seed (peas, beans)
  - Stem (asparagus, celery)
  - Root (carrots, potatoes)

- Take the Garden in the Box or go out to your garden and ask the children to **identify** the vegetables that have been planted into at least **two groups/families** for **3-4yr olds, two or three groups** for **4-5yr olds** and **four family groups** for children aged **5 and up**.

Next ask children to think of **movements** that can **personify families of vegetables** or even **specific vegetables**, to help children **identify** and **remember** the different **types of vegetables**. For example, bulb vegetables can be represented by positioning your arms into hoops. For jumping beans you can jump up and down, and for runner beans, run on the spot. Rehearse the moves you invented before playing ***Mr Potato***, track 8 of The Vegetable Plot CD.

Ask the students to turn to the *Vegetable Families* activity, pages 22 and 23 in their journal, and **categorize the vegetables** on the opposite page by **drawing** them in the chart. Answers can be found on page 145.

## Math

*How many [bulb/flower/fruit/leaf/root/stem/seed] vegetables can you count in each family group?*

**All Ages**

- Prepare a basket containing a **variety of vegetable** types and ask the children to **sort** through them based on the family types you have just reviewed. Once sorted by **family types**, **count** each vegetable out loud to find out how many vegetables are in each **group**.

Repeat the activity to categorize and count the vegetable plants used in the Garden in the Box or garden and **complete** the classroom **Vegetable Families Chart** found on page 144.

Ask the children to **complete** *My Family Tree* on page 24 of their journals to **link** the **concept** of their **own family** to that of a vegetable family.

## Arts

*What different sounds can we make from our shakers?*
*What other instruments can we make from vegetables?*

**All Ages**

- **Encourage** children's **creativity** by asking them to think of as **many ideas** as possible for different **uses for vegetables** (other than eating). Look up the **Vienna Vegetable Orchestra** online to get inspired by the ways professional musicians have found to play vegetables as instruments.

- Prepare to make a **Pepper Shaker** by cutting around the stalk of a few different colored peppers (one per child or per group of 3-4 children) and removing the 'lid' of the pepper. **Remove the seeds** (keep) and the rest of the insides of the pepper, being careful not to pierce the side of the pepper.

- Ask the children to fill the **pepper** with **rice** and cover with the lid. Hold on to the lid and shake the pepper to make sound. For younger children, you may want to secure the lid with tape to avoid accidents. Repeat with lighter materials (such as the seeds that were extracted). **Experiment** with different contents and see what happens to the **sound**. Smaller, more dense items like rice make higher-pitched sounds, whereas lighter, hollower materials make a lower sound.

**5yrs+**

- Have other vegetables and materials (for example, rubber bands, etc.) available for children aged 5 and up to experiment with.

**Play** the *Mr Potato* song (track 8) again, and this time play along with your vegetable instruments. You can group the children by families of vegetables!

**Teacher's Tips**
Consider using the leftover vegetables from your vegetable orchestra for your class compost.

## Observations

## Vegetable Families Chart

| VEGETABLE FAMILY | Draw vegetables | Draw vegetables | Draw vegetables | Draw vegetables |
|---|---|---|---|---|
| **Flower**  | | | | |
| **Fruit**  | | | | |
| **Leaf**  | | | | |
| **Root**  | | | | |

## Vegetable Families: Answer Key

| VEGETABLE FAMILY | Draw vegetables | Draw vegetables | Draw vegetables | Draw vegetables |
|---|---|---|---|---|
| **Flower** |  Zucchini flower |  Cauliflower |  Artichoke |  Broccoli |
| **Fruit** |  Tomato |  Eggplant |  Zucchini |  Okra |
| **Leaf** |  Spinach |  Lettuce |  Rocket |  Basil |
| **Root** |  Potato | 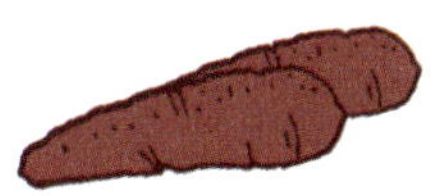 Cassava |  Beet |  Arracacha |

# How Did Your Vegetables Grow?

*Describing matured and harvested vegetables with the use of prepositions and comparative adjectives.*

This lesson is about identifying plants' cues to know when the produce is ripe and ready to be picked! Prior to picking the produce, children are encouraged to use language to express mathematical concepts such as positions, shape and size, and prepositions to describe how the vegetables have grown. They also learn how to identify when a vegetable is ready to be picked (ripe) and to be eaten through their sense of touch.

**Science & Nature**

**Wonder**
- Carrots and Cassava p. 24
- Squeeze Your Vegetables p. 25

**Observation**
- Developing My Sense of Taste p. 27

**Investigation**
- Above and Under the Ground p. 25

**Vocabulary**
Prepositions: above, behind, between, down, in, inside, near, over, under, with
Comparative adjectives: bigger than, smaller than, the same as

*Squeeze Your Vegetables*, (track 6)
*Herbs and Spices*, (track 11)

<table>
<tr><th>ACTIVITY</th><th>SKILLS</th><th>MATERIALS</th><th>JOURNALS</th></tr>
<tr><td>Science & Nature<br>All Ages<br>• Identification of the plants' cues to know when its produce is ready to be picked or dug up</td><td>• Developing spatial awareness<br>• Identifying how vegetables grow and their size.</td><td>• Garden in the Box or plants from the garden<br>• The Vegetable Plot CD, Squeeze Your Vegetables, track 6</td><td>W • Carrots and Cassava p. 24<br>• Squeeze Your Vegetables p. 25<br>I • Above and Under the Ground p. 25</td></tr>
<tr><td>Science & Nature<br>All Ages<br>• Preparation and tasting of Gazpacho</td><td>• Developing a sense of taste by distinguishing sweet from sour<br>• Developing fine motor skills by mixing ingredients in a bowl</td><td>• 1 cup chopped onion<br>• 1 cup chopped tomato<br>• 1 cup finely chopped bell pepper<br>• 1 cup chopped carrot<br>• 1 cup chopped olives<br>• 1 cup chopped parsley and green onion/chives<br>• 1 cup raw cassava flour<br>• 1 cup corn flour<br>• 1 cup olive oil<br>• 3 hard boiled eggs<br>• Pinch of salt<br>• Pinch of oregano<br>• The Vegetable Plot CD, Herbs and Spices, track 11</td><td>O • Developing My Sense of Taste p. 27</td></tr>
</table>

## Guiding Questions

**Our Green Question**
*How do we know when a vegetable is ready to be harvested?*

## Before and During the Lesson

- How do [*carrots/radishes/potatoes/tomatoes/onions/celery, etc*] grow?
- Why do you think it's important to group vegetables into families?
- What can we do with our hands to see if a vegetable is ready to be picked?

## End of Lesson Reflection

- What's a fruit or vegetable that's popular in the summer?
- What types of soup do we eat in the winter? Why is that?
- Do vegetables all have the same flavors?

## Science & Nature

*What signs can we see when a vegetable is ready to be picked?*
*What meals or snacks can we make with vegetables?*

### All Ages

- **Review** some of the following tips to know **when your produce is ripe** and ready to be picked:
    - **Eggplants**: These are ready to harvest when they are full size with glossy skin. They should be cut off the plant instead of picked.
    - **Beets**: This vegetable can be harvested when its diameter is about 4 cm or more.
    - **Baby carrots**: Pick these when the shoulders are 2cm thick and the color is an intense shade of orange.
    - **Zucchinis**: These should be picked when they are 15-20cm long, dark green in color, and have a firm texture.
    - **Cucumbers**: These are ready when they are full size with small seeds and shiny skin.
    - **Lettuces**: Use scissors to cut the lettuces when they are about 10 - 12 cm tall. Cut them to about 5 cm above the ground.
    - **Onions**: Young onions should be harvested when they are 20 cm - 30 cm tall.
    - **Peas**: Peas can be picked at different stages depending on your preferences. For developed peas, allow more time than for edible hulls and pick them when the pods begin to look swollen.
    - **Radishes**: We should pick radishes before the root has a diameter of 2 cm. Radishes mature at different speeds depending on whether they were planted in spring/summer or winter.
    - **Spinach**: Once a spinach plant has grown about 6 leaves, you can start to pick them. Make sure to leave a minimum of 4 leaves on the plant to help it to regrow. Spinach can also be cut with scissors to 3 cm above the ground when it is about 12 - 15 cm tall.
    - **Tomatoes**: A tomato can be picked before it is completely ripe as it needs some time to ripen off the vine too. Pick them when they are a darkish green color and some parts are beginning to turn light red.

Play the song *Squeeze Your Vegetables* (track 6) from The Vegetable Plot CD and listen for different indicators to know when a vegetable is ready to be picked.

W Some vegetables grow **above** the **ground**, like **tomatoes** and **peas**. Ask the children to find the squeezed vegetables and finger paint the seeds inside on the *Squeeze Your Vegetables* activity on page 25 of your journal. Point out the fact that the edible parts of other plants grow **under** the **ground**, like carrots and cassava, so it is harder to know when they are ready to be harvested, as you can only see their leaves. Turn to the *Carrots and Cassava* activity on page 24 of the journal and handprint the leaves above the ground to complete the vegetables.

I Complete the *Above and Under the Ground* activity on page 25 by looking for the plants' cues and drawing the carrot, tomatoes, cassava, and onion in their journal.

## Science & Nature

*Which fresh seasonal vegetables complement each other in flavor?*

## Teacher Set-Up

- Gather the ingredients for the *Raw Farofa*. Peel and chop the onions, tomato, bell pepper, carrot, olives, parsley and green onions or chives. Check for any allergies beforehand.

### Raw Farofa

*Ingredients*

1 cup chopped onion
1 cup chopped tomato
1 cup finely chopped bell pepper
1 cup chopped carrot
1 cup chopped olives
1 cup chopped parsley and green onion/chives
1 cup raw cassava flour
1 cup corn flour
1 cup olive oil
3 hard boiled eggs
Pinch of salt
Pinch of oregano

### All Ages

Introducing children to **cooking** is a key element to *The Garden Project* as it links the growing and harvesting activities to healthy eating. Prior to organizing children into smaller groups, play *Herbs and Spices* (track 11) from The Vegetable Plot CD to get into the groove of making this recipe.

- **Farofa** is a toasted cassava and/or corn flour mixture that is commonly served with meats in Brazil. This is a raw variation that is not toasted and uses fresh vegetables that are prepared and eaten raw, which makes it easy to do with children in the classroom.

- Take the vegetables you diced earlier and have the children work together to toss them into a large bowl, taking turns to stir the ingredients together. Add the cassava and corn flour to the mixture together with the hard-boiled eggs and olive oil. Taste it and adjust the salt accordingly. If you wish, add other spices. Refrigerate.

- Serve the Farofa in bowls.

0 Ask the children to taste the **tomatoes** (sweet) and **green pepper** (sour) and ask them about what **taste sensations** and **textures** these vegetables have. Turn to the *Developing My Sense of Taste* activity on page 27 and ask the children to draw the vegetable they tasted next to its corresponding taste sensation. Additionally, ask them to complete the color association they had when tasting it.

**Teacher's Tips**
Repeat this lesson whenever you see there are vegetables in your garden or Garden in the Box that are ready to be picked.

## Observations

# Eating by Season

*Children learn that there is a reason and a season for everything.*

Just like humans, plants need water, food, and sunshine to grow. And just like us, every plant has different sun, rain, food, and temperature needs. In this lesson, we will review the seasonality of fruit and vegetables.

Learning there is a season and a reason for everything is a very valuable lesson for children to learn early in life! In addition, one of the primary goals for *The Garden Project* is to introduce healthy eating habits to young children. If they know how to make healthy choices from a young age, this habit will stay with them for a lifetime.

**Science & Nature**

**W Wonder**
- At the Market p. 26

**O Observation**
- Fruit and Vegetable Color Wheel p. 28
- Seasonal Fruit and Vegetable Cut-outs p. 37

**I Investigation**
- My Harvest Chart pp. 26-27

**Vocabulary**
January, February, March, April, May, June, July, August, September, October, November, December, harvest, fruit, vegetables

*Mango,* (track 7)

# > Lesson Overview

| ACTIVITY | SKILLS | MATERIALS | JOURNALS |
| --- | --- | --- | --- |
| **Science & Nature**<br>**All Ages**<br>• Completion of the classroom Harvest Chart by coloring the squares in the chart<br>• Establishing a link between seasonal fruit and vegetables and vegetables that are ready to be harvested from the garden | • *Identification of seasonal fruit and vegetables*<br>• *Completing a chart*<br>• *Developing early numeracy skills through counting different fruit and vegetables*<br>• *Gently harvesting seasonal vegetables* | • Our Harvest Chart Poster<br>• Vegetable cut-outs<br>• Garden in the Box or plants from the garden | W • At the Market p. 26<br>I • My Harvest Chart pp. 26-27 |
| **Science & Nature**<br>**4-5yrs**<br>• Introduction of different colored fruit and vegetables and link with the color wheel<br>**All Ages**<br>• Preparation and tasting of a Garden Salad | • *Grouping images of fruit and vegetables by color groups*<br>• *Identifying the primary ingredients of a salad*<br>• *Fine motor skills for mixing ingredients together in a bowl* | • Seasonal Vegetable cut-outs<br>• Scissors<br>• Glue<br>• The Vegetable Plot CD, *Mango*, track 7<br>Ingredients for the Garden Salad:<br>• 100g of rocket<br>• 100g of iceberg lettuce<br>• 100g of romaine lettuce<br>• Tomatoes (sundried if not in season)<br>• 1 Lemon<br>• Olive oil<br>• Pinch of salt<br>Optional vegetables and cheese:<br>• Mango<br>• Cucumber<br>• Whole small peppers (pimenta biquinho)<br>• Palm hearts<br>• Baby broccoli<br>• 1 Radish<br>• ½ Beet<br>• Sliced avocado<br>• Crumbled cheese | O • Seasonal Fruit and Vegetable Cut-outs p. 37<br>• Fruit and Vegetable Color Wheel p. 28 |

## Guiding Questions

**Our Green Question**
*Why do fruit and vegetables mature at different times of the year?*

## Before and During the Lesson

- When do your favorite vegetables mature?
- Why do you think there are different vegetables available at different times of the year?
- How do you think the plant knows what season it is in?

## End of Lesson Reflection

- Do you think you could "trick" the plant into believing it's in a different season? If so, how? (Think about vegetables that are grown in greenhouses or given UV lighting).
- Do you know any fruit and vegetables that come from different parts of the world?
- Do you know any fruit and vegetables that come from your country?

## Teacher Set-Up

- Wash, peel, and chop up fresh **seasonal vegetables**, such as tomatoes, cucumbers, radishes, small peppers, palm hearts, baby broccoli, and beets, and put each ingredient into small separate bowls.

## Science & Nature

*Which fruit and vegetables do you harvest in [month/season]? What is your favorite vegetable?*

### All Ages

- Pin up the *Our Harvest Chart* poster and review the fact that every vegetable has its own different timing and needs. Some plants need more sun and warmer temperatures than others and therefore they ripen at different times of the year.

Observe the vegetables in your garden or Garden in the Box and see which ones are ready to be harvested. Color the square in the corresponding month of the classroom **Our Harvest Chart**.

W Link the seasonality of the plants in your garden or Garden in the Box with the fruit and vegetables that are available at the farmer's market. Ask the children to complete the *At the Market* activity on page 26 of their journals, identifying the colors of the fruit and practicing counting the items.

I Older children are able to do the Harvest Chart activity individually on their personal *My Harvest Chart* on pages 26 and 27 of their journal.

**Teacher's Tips**

Watch videos of fruit and vegetables being harvested to give children an idea of how fruit and vegetables are collected. Be sure to explain that harvesting times change according to the country, climate, and continent they are in.

## Science & Nature

*How do you know if a food is healthy? What are some of the healthiest foods we can eat?*

### 4-5yrs

- Highlight the fact that fruit and vegetables have **vibrant colors**, especially before they are cooked. Generally speaking, the brighter the colors of fruit and vegetables, the better they are for our bodies.

O Now turn to the *Seasonal Fruit and Vegetables* cut-outs on page 37 at the back of the journals and ask children to **identify** which of them are currently **in season**. Children **cut out** the shapes and turn to the *Fruit and Vegetable Color Wheel* on page 28 of their journals. Ask them to **match** the **cut-outs** with the fruit and vegetables on their **wheel**. **Add the missing ones** with the corresponding colored cut-out and ask the children which of these fruit and vegetables could be used to make a **salad**.

### All Ages

Play *Mango*, track 7 from The Vegetable Plot CD, to introduce the task of **making a salad** as a very **healthy** recipe which **combines** a large variety of **uncooked vegetables** in a dish or tasty meal.

- **Talk** about how **good** it is for your body to **eat salad** because it has a lot of **fresh** and **raw ingredients** in it. Remind children that **lettuce** is one of the **easiest** and **quickest** things to **harvest**. Now it's your turn to make a salad!

**Garden Salad**
*Ingredients*
100g of rocket
100g of iceberg lettuce
100g of romaine lettuce
Tomatoes (sundried if not in season)
1 Lemon
Olive oil
Pinch of salt

Optional seasonal ingredients:
Cucumber
Whole small peppers (pimenta biquinho)
Palm hearts
Baby broccoli
1 Radish
½ Beet
1 Mango
Sliced avocado
Crumbled cheese

- Ask children to **choose the tender leaves** of the **mixed greens** or salad you planted in the Garden in the Box or garden. Mixed greens can be picked as tiny 5cm baby *thinnings* and you can start harvesting the outer leaves as soon as the plants have at least 5 to 6 full-size leaves. Wash the leaves under running water and dry.

- Take the **fresh seasonal vegetables** you prepared and **put** into a **large bowl** and **add the salad leaves**.

- In a small bowl, **squeeze the lemon**, **and mix** the **juice**, **olive oil**, and **salt** together then pour the **mixture** into the salad and **toss** it all together. **Serve** the salad to each participating child and eat!

- Ask the children to **identify** the **colors** in their **salad**.

## Observations

## Our Harvest Chart

This chart demonstrates the seasonality of fruits and vegetables in a tropical climate with cold and dry winters, such as the South-East of Brazil, and will vary depending on your region and climate. If in doubt, research online or ask at a local garden shop or plant nursery.

| CROP NAME | JAN | FEB | MAR | APRIL | MAY | JUNE | JULY | AUG | SEPT | OCT | NOV | DEC |
|---|---|---|---|---|---|---|---|---|---|---|---|---|
| Beets | ✓ | ✓ | ✓ | ✓ | ✓ | | | ✓ | ✓ | ✓ | ✓ | ✓ |
| Carrots | ✓ | ✓ | ✓ | ✓ | ✓ | ✓ | ✓ | ✓ | ✓ | ✓ | ✓ | ✓ |
| Lettuce | ✓ | ✓ | ✓ | ✓ | ✓ | ✓ | ✓ | ✓ | ✓ | ✓ | ✓ | ✓ |
| Okra | ✓ | ✓ | ✓ | | | | | | | | | |
| Onions | | | | | | | ✓ | ✓ | ✓ | ✓ | ✓ | ✓ |
| Peppers | | | | | | | ✓ | ✓ | ✓ | ✓ | ✓ | ✓ |
| Potatoes | ✓ | ✓ | ✓ | ✓ | | | | | | | | ✓ |
| Radishes | ✓ | ✓ | ✓ | ✓ | ✓ | ✓ | ✓ | ✓ | ✓ | ✓ | ✓ | ✓ |
| Spinach | ✓ | ✓ | ✓ | ✓ | ✓ | ✓ | ✓ | ✓ | ✓ | ✓ | ✓ | ✓ |
| Strawberries | | | | | | ✓ | ✓ | ✓ | ✓ | | | |
| Tomatoes | ✓ | | | | | | | ✓ | ✓ | ✓ | ✓ | ✓ |

# Eating the Rainbow!

*Developing healthy eating habits.*

This lesson looks at drawing a parallel between brightly colored fruit and vegetables and their high nutritional value. In fact, the most nutritional foods are those that are eaten raw and keep their bright colors.

We want to make it easy for children to make healthy eating choices. Children will remember the colors of fruit and vegetables, identifying what they look like by shape and color and discover the colors of the rainbow as they color their plate! In addition, they will understand that different colors have different nutritional values.

**Science & Nature**

**Arts**

**Wonder**
- Colorful Vegetables p. 27

**Observation**
- Eating the Rainbow! p. 29
- My Favorite Recipe p. 30
- What's for Dinner? p. 31

**Investigation**
- Creative Juices p. 28
- Fruit Mandalas p. 29
- Fruit Thaumatrope p. 30

**Vocabulary**
eat, sleep, exercise, balance, diet, colors of the rainbow, rainbow, apples, sun, flowers, grass, grapes, carrots, sky

*Artie's Community Garden,* (track 10)

| ACTIVITY | SKILLS | MATERIALS | JOURNALS |
| --- | --- | --- | --- |
| **Science & Nature**<br>**All Ages**<br>• Introduction and revision of the five fruit and vegetable color groups: red, orange/yellow, green, white/brown and purple/blue<br>• Balance of different colored vegetables on a paper plate | • *Identifying healthy foods by color, combining foods to make nutritious snacks*<br>• *Developing hand-eye coordination through coloring* | • Paper plates<br>• An assortment of seasonal fruit and vegetables in many different colors<br>• Colored pencils or crayons<br>• The Vegetable Plot CD, *Artie's Community Garden*, track 10 | W • Colorful Vegetables p. 27<br>O • Eating the Rainbow! p. 29<br>• My Favorite Recipe p. 30<br>• What's for Dinner? p. 31 |
| **Arts**<br>**5yrs+**<br>• Observation and completion of the orange mandala<br>• Transformation of the mandala into an orange thaumatrope<br>**Project Ideas**<br>**5yrs+**<br>• Introduction of new ways to eat fresh, seasonal fruit through smoothies<br>• Documentation of smoothie concoctions | • *Observing and demonstrating pattern awareness in nature*<br>• *Constructing a simple pattern when prompted*<br>• *Making a simple animation by blending two images into one*<br>• *Developing imagination through smoothie concoctions* | *Fruit Mandalas and Thaumatrope*<br>• Colored pencils or crayons, orange<br>• Scissors<br>• String<br>*Fruit Smoothies*<br>• Assortment of fresh, seasonal fruit<br>• Plain yogurt<br>• Maple syrup (if unavailable, use honey)<br>• Ice<br>• Vanilla (optional) | I • Creative Juices p. 28<br>• Fruit Mandalas p. 29<br>• Fruit Thaumatrope p. 30 |

## Guiding Questions

**Our Green Question**
*Why is it important to eat a variety of colored fruit and vegetables?*

## Before and During the Lesson

- How do you know if a fruit or vegetable is good for you?
- When are fruits and vegetables most tasty?
- What other ways can you eat fresh seasonal fruit and vegetables?

## End of Lesson Reflection

- What is a balanced diet, relating to fruit and vegetables?
- How can you make sure that you have more of a balanced diet?
- What are your favorite ways to eat fruit and vegetables?

## Science & Nature

*Can you name a fruit and vegetable for each color group? Why should we eat a variety of different colored vegetables?*

**All Ages**

- **Show** the children the **fruit and vegetables** you have prepared for this lesson. If possible, use fruit and vegetables you have **harvested** from the Garden in the Box or garden. If you don't have enough for this activity, use **seasonal** fruit and vegetables.

- Ask the children to point out what **colors** the fruit and vegetables are. **Distribute** one **paper/plastic plate** per child together with a **variety** of **fruit and vegetables** in an assortment of colors. Talk about the fact that it is best to eat fruit and vegetables **raw** (making sure that they are edible when raw). This is when they are **brightest** and **most nutritious**.

- Next explain that it's important to have a **balance** of **colors** on your **plate**. If there is too much of one color, add another fruit or vegetable of a different color. Now use the ***Fruit and Vegetable Color Wheel*** on page 163 to show children that fruit and vegetables can be **categorized** into **five color groups**: red, orange/yellow, green, blue/purple and brown/white.

- Ask the children to **choose** the **fruit and vegetables** to make a **composition** on their paper plates based on the **color wheel**. Ask them to use as many different colored fruits as possible for a "balanced" plate and be sure to point out if there are too many fruit or vegetables of one color.

Play *Artie's Community Garden*, track 10 of The Vegetable Plot CD, and play along with the song. Ask the children to listen for the names of fruit and vegetables and when they hear one to point to its color on the Color Wheel.

W — Ask the children to **complete** the *Colorful Vegetables* activity on page 27 of their journal by **coloring** their vegetables with ***vibrant colors*** (carrot = orange, tomato = red, sweetcorn = yellow, potatoes = brown, eggplant = purple and okra = green).

O — Remind the children of the **color wheel** and ask them to complete the plate of colorful vegetables on the *Eating the Rainbow!* activity on page 29 of their journal.

Next, ask the children to create their favorite recipe using an assortment of different colored fruit and vegetables. Ask them to **document** the ingredients on the *My Favorite Recipe* activity on page 30 of their journal and share their finished recipe on page 31, *What's for Dinner?*

## Arts

*How are the colors and patterns different on the inside and outside? Are the colors/patterns the same?*

**5yrs+**

- Children are more likely to taste foods if they have had the chance to **manipulate them**. This activity highlights the natural beauty that can be found in fruit. **Select** a number of **fresh fruits** that show beautiful patterns when cut in half, such as an orange or kiwi. These **repeated patterns** are natural ***mandalas***.

I — Complete the *Fruit Mandalas* on page 29 of the journal, then make the *Thaumatrope* on page 30. A **thaumatrope** is a toy from the 19th Century. It's made by securing two pieces of string to a disc with a different image on each side. By quickly spinning the strings between their fingers, children can create an optical illusion that 'blends' the two images into one. This allows children to begin experimenting with a **basic animation technique**.

## Project Ideas

*What other creative ways can you eat fresh, seasonal fruit?*

**5yrs+**

- There are many ways in which you can **introduce** eating **fresh seasonal fruit**. One of these is by making **smoothies**, which are hugely popular with many children, even those who claim not to like fruit or yogurt.

### Fresh Fruit Smoothies

Assortment of fresh, seasonal fruit
Plain yogurt
Maple syrup (if unavailable, honey)
Ice
Vanilla (optional)

- Select a **couple of seasonal fruits** and **blend** together with **ice**, **yogurt** or **even frozen yogurt**. Add a splash of vanilla and a drizzle of **honey** or **maple syrup** to sweeten the smoothie up. *Insider tip: Freeze ripe or overripe peeled bananas in a freezer bag bag to use in future smoothies.*

Ask the children to **color** their **concoctions** on the *Creative Juices* activity on page 28 of their journal.

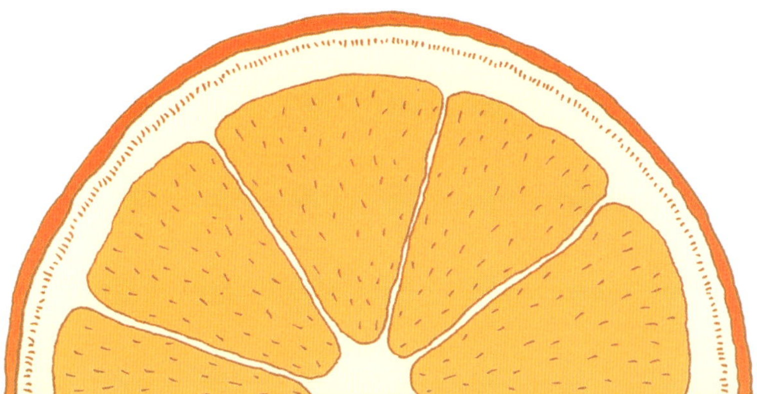

## Observations

## End of Year Project

# Seed You Next Year

This end of year project was conceived to be done optionally with children of all ages to give closure to The Garden Project for the year. Ultimately, we want children to understand that a plant's purpose is to produce and disseminate its seeds, so that it can keep its life going.

In this end of year project, children extract and prepare the seeds from their harvested fruit and vegetables to prepare for next year's garden. This project also acts as a wonderful link between classes and/or academic years, as the children's experience can be encapsulated into the seeds that are passed on and will become the seeds for the incoming class.

### Project Goals

- Understanding the cyclical essence of nature
- Appreciating seeds and their role in renewing life
- Recognizing that seeds can be preserved in many ways
- Learning that seeds have to be thoroughly washed before they can be preserved

# Seed You Next Year

*Find out how plants continue their life cycle through seeds.*

Plants and trees need to spread their seeds so that they can continue their life cycle. Different plants have evolved different mechanisms for dispersing their seeds and some are very smart! A favorite is the dandelion, whose clocks of individual seeds and their parachutes are lifted and blown away on the lightest breeze.

In this end of year project, we are going to extract and gather the seeds from the fruit and vegetables we harvested and put them into little seed packs ready to be seeded and grown next year!

Seed-saving is an essential part of gardening and, over time, what makes your garden truly your own. Prepare a pack of seeds for next year's class as a way to link the learning from one academic year to the next!

Engineering

Science & Nature

Arts

**Vocabulary**
Seeds, harvesting, plant cycle, germination, types of seeds, adjectives describing seeds (small, round, light, heavy, smooth, rough)

*Pyjamazon Jungle,*
(track 12)

# > End of Year Project Overview

| ACTIVITY | SKILLS | MATERIALS |
|---|---|---|
| **Engineering**<br>**All Ages**<br>• Collection of seeds on a nature walk<br><br>**5yrs+**<br>• Highlight the smart ways plants spread their seeds by using sample seeds and experimentation | • *Identifying a variety of dispersal modes*<br>• *Experimenting with seeds*<br>• *Devising ways for seeds to move* | • A variety of different types of seeds<br>• Organic bell pepper seeds<br>• Loose parts, such as cardboard rolls, twigs<br>• Glue, tape, or any sticky agent (child safe)<br>• Scissors, for older children<br>• Earthy clay<br>• Compost<br>• Water |
| **Science & Nature**<br>**All Ages**<br>• Extraction of seasonal and pepper seeds to be stored in seed packs for the following year<br><br>**Project Ideas**<br>**5yrs+**<br>• Germination and observation of an avocado to keep as a classroom plant | • *Understanding the concept that fruit and vegetables continue their life cycle through the seeds they produce*<br>• *Identifying the stages in extracting seeds for future storage*<br>• *Observing the process of germination* | • Fruit and vegetables with seeds from the garden or Garden in the Box<br>• Bell peppers or pumpkins<br>• Paper towels<br>• Bowl<br>• Sieve<br>• The Vegetable Plot CD, *Pyjamazon Jungle*, track 12<br><br>Avocado Extraction<br>• Avocado pits, 1 per child<br>• Toothpicks, 3 per pit<br>• Glass tumbler or small bowl<br>• Small pot of compost soil (later) |
| **Arts**<br>**4yrs+**<br>• Creation of a seed library from the harvested seeds, stored in brown paper bags | • *Designing seed packets*<br>• *Identifying symbols that can be used to provide information about how to grow and care for the plant* | • Seeds harvested from fruit or vegetables<br>• Images or cut-outs of vegetables<br>• Glue<br>• Scissors<br>• Crayons or markers, many colors<br>• Brown paper bags |

## Guiding Questions

**Our Green Question**
*Why do fruit and vegetables have seeds?*

## Before and During the Lesson

- Can you think of ways for your seeds to travel?
- How can we remove (extract) seeds from vegetables to store them for the following year?
- Where can we put the seeds if we aren't going to re-plant them right away?

## End of Lesson Reflection

- Why are most seeds small?
- Which seeds went the farthest and why?
- What additional information should be added on the seed packets so next year's class knows how to grow them?

**Teacher's Tip**
Plants and trees need to spread their seeds and have found a number of smart ways to do this. Head outdoors and see if you can find different types of seeds: self-dispersal (pepper pots, exploders), wind dispersal (parachutes, spinners) and animal/bird dispersal (sticky seeds and tasty seeds).

## Engineering

*How do plants move their seeds from one place to another?*

### All Ages

- Go on a **nature walk** to collect a variety of seeds in the garden or park. Plants have very little **mobility**, which means that they cannot move around like us. They don´t have feet or legs, so they have to rely on a variety of ways to disperse (move). Try to collect a **sample of seeds** that use a variety of forms of dispersal: ***gravity, wind, ballistic*** *(through an* ***explosion of water*** *and through* ***animals*** *(us).* Explain that a plant's goal is to grow a flower and/or fruit so that it can make new seeds and then disperse its seeds in order to continue its life cycle through another plant.

- Once back in the classroom, demonstrate various ways that we can move seeds from one place to another. **Split** children into **smaller groups** and have them **test** the various ways, experimenting with different ways, air (blowing) or gravity (dropping them), for example.

### 5yrs+

- Now hand out two **types of seeds: beans** and **bell pepper seeds**. Ask them to **devise** ways for vegetables to be transported from one place to the other. Have materials available to extend the experimentation: sticks, glue, tape, cardboard rolls. Observe the ingenious outcomes the children come up with. Whose seed can travel the furthest?

- To add a **tactile dimension** to this activity, turn your seeds into **seed bombs** by taking a **handful of seeds** and **mixing them** with soil, clay and water and **rolling them** into **balls** until firm and hard. Students of all ages will thoroughly enjoy this activity. Seed bombs were designed to enable seeds to be sown in hard to reach places, and in locations where a gardener is unable to spend long periods of time preparing the ground for conventional sowing.

## Science & Nature

*How can we regrow our Garden in the Box next year from this season's harvest?*

### All Ages

- **Explain** that **seeds** generally come from a **plant's fruit** or ***seed head*** that develops after the plant goes to flower (leafy greens, and root vegetables flower and then form seed heads, so it is unlikely you will be harvesting these types of seeds unless you have given these plants ample time to flower).

- Have a **sample** of **fruit vegetables** you've grown from the Garden in the Box or garden with **seeds** that can **easily be extracted**. Supplement with a **selection of bell peppers**, in a variety of colors. Be sure to select a variety that have seeds. Organic is ideal as most supermarket peppers are picked before they are ripe, meaning the seeds are unlikely to grow. It is crucial that the vegetables you choose are ripe before you extract the seeds or pits or they will not grow.

- Give a seedpod or ripe fruit vegetable to each child and ask the children to **extract the seeds** using **child-friendly tweezers** or **popsicle sticks**. Once extracted, **wash off** the seeds **thoroughly**, making sure they are completely clean. For pumpkins, extract the pits, scrape the seeds of the fruit and wash well in a sieve, rubbing all traces of the flesh thoroughly.

- Put the seeds between **moist paper towels** and then **transfer** the seeds to a **bowl** or plate and let them **air dry**. Once dry, **put them into** a small brown paper bag.

Play *Pyjamazon Jungle*, track 12 of The Vegetable Plot CD as the children are extracting their seeds. Just like macaws shape the forest by spreading some seeds and destroying others, **imagine** being **a wild animal** that is **seeding** the **Amazon Rainforest** with magical seeds.

**5yrs+**

- Ask children to turn the seed packs and **add the date** on the **back** of the paper bag. Add information about the **care needed** for the seeds, what time of year to plant, and when to harvest with **symbols**, for example two suns can represent a plant that needs lots of sunlight and one drop of water a plant that doesn't need to be watered very often.

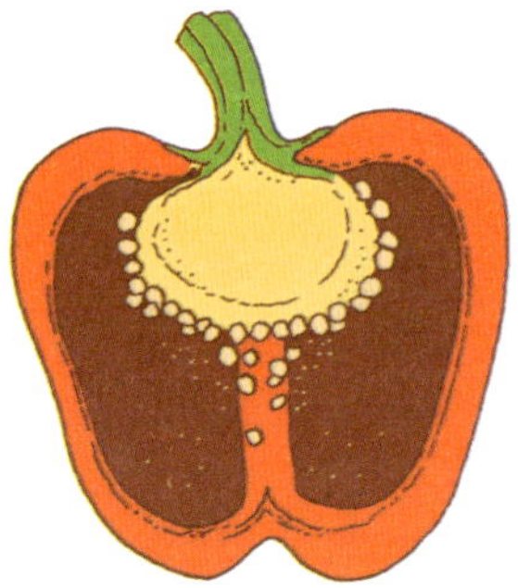

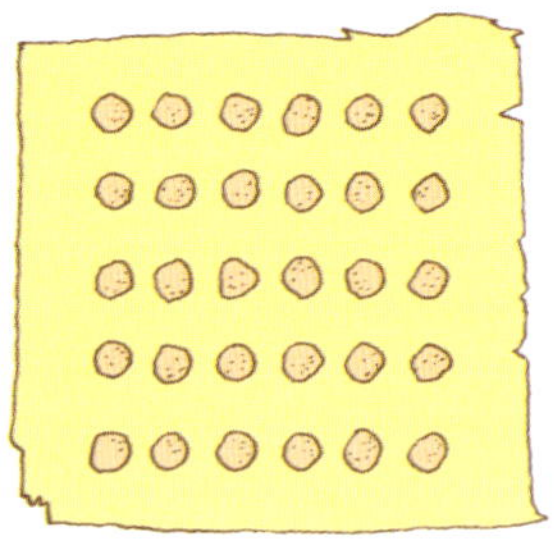

## Arts

*Which pictures and colors can we use on seed packets to show what plant will grow?*

- Create a **seed library** of the vegetables that were grown by repeating the previous activity to extract the seeds. Start by finding out if your seeds are still good to plant by putting your seeds in a glass of water. If they sink, they're good; if they float, throw them away.

- Hand a **brown paper bag** to each child and ask the children to draw or **glue** cut-outs or pictures of the fruit and vegetables seeds you will store on the front of the seed pack (small brown paper bag).

## Observations

# W Specialized Science & Nature Skills Assessment

**WONDER**

Use these statements to assess the hands-on science and nature skills that have been developed during the project.

| ✓ | EQUIPMENT SKILLS |
|---|---|
| | I can pour water slowly using a rain cup or light container |
| | I can dig a hole using a small trowel or spade |

| ✓ | PLANTING SKILLS |
|---|---|
| | I can sow large seeds, such as a lima bean or seed bomb |
| | I can dig up the earth |
| | I can fill a cup with soil |
| | I can put a plant in a hole that I dug up |
| | I can firm in a plant in with help |

| ✓ | AFTER-CARE SKILLS |
|---|---|
| | I can water seedlings |
| | I can water established plants |

| ✓ | HARVESTING SKILLS |
|---|---|
| | I can dig root crops, such as carrots and radishes, without damaging them |
| | I can identify when some vegetables are ripe by squeezing them lightly |
| | I can delicately pick a ripe vegetable from its branch, for example a cherry tomato |

| ✓ | OTHER SKILLS |
|---|---|
| | I can identify the natural elements that a plant needs to survive |
| | I can identify one or two seasons |
| | I can describe the texture of natural elements and materials |
| | I can identify one or two bugs/creatures that can be found in a garden |

| ✓ | FINE MOTOR SKILLS |
|---|---|
| | I can represent a flower using squiggly lines |
| | I can use a cork or cotton for printing |
| | I can glue natural materials on paper |

Teacher's comments

# O Specialized Science & Nature Skills Assessment

## OBSERVATION

Use these statements to assess the hands-on science and nature skills that have been developed during the project.

| ✓ | EQUIPMENT SKILLS |
|---|---|
| | I can use a watering can to water plants |
| | I can use a measuring stick to measure plant growth |

| ✓ | PLANTING SKILLS |
|---|---|
| | I can sow large seeds such as lima beans |
| | I can sow medium seeds such as spinach |
| | I can sow fine seeds such as tomatoes, coriander, and lettuce |
| | I can fill a container ready for sowing |
| | I can fill a cup with soil |
| | I can remove a young plant from its container |
| | I can plant a young plant into the soil and firm in |

| ✓ | AFTER-CARE SKILLS |
|---|---|
| | I can water seedlings |
| | I can water established plants |
| | I can pinch out plants such as sweet peas, broad beans, and tomatoes |

| ✓ | HARVESTING SKILLS |
|---|---|
| | I can dig root crops, such as carrots and radishes, without damaging them |
| | I can harvest leafy crops, such as lettuce and spinach, without damaging the plant |

| ✓ | OTHER SKILLS |
|---|---|
| | I can conduct hand texturing tests of soil to determine soil type |
| | I can sow small seeds such as radish seeds |
| | I can distinguish sweet from sour |
| | I can observe the changes in plants, fruit, and vegetables |

| ✓ | PLANNING SKILLS |
|---|---|
| | I can draw my garden plan |
| | I can choose plants to grow |

| ✓ | RE-PLANTING SKILLS |
|---|---|
| | I can start my new vegetable garden by extracting seeds from harvested vegetables and storing them to plant the following year. |

Teacher's comments

# I Specialized Science & Nature Skills Assessment

## INVESTIGATION

Use these statements to assess the hands-on science and nature skills that have been developed during the project.

| ✓ | EQUIPMENT SKILLS |
|---|---|
| | I can use a watering can to water plants |
| | I can use a measuring stick to measure plant growth |

| ✓ | PLANTING SKILLS |
|---|---|
| | I can sow large seeds such as lima beans |
| | I can sow medium seeds such as spinach |
| | I can sow fine seeds such as tomatoes, coriander, and lettuce |
| | I can fill a container ready for sowing |
| | I can fill a cup with soil |
| | I can remove a young plant from its container |
| | I can plant a young plant into the soil and firm in |

| ✓ | AFTER-CARE SKILLS |
|---|---|
| | I can water seedlings |
| | I can water established plants |
| | I can pinch out plants such as sweet peas, broad beans, and tomatoes |

| ✓ | HARVESTING SKILLS |
|---|---|
| | I can dig root crops, such as carrots and radishes, without damaging them |
| | I can harvest leafy crops, such as lettuce and spinach, without damaging the plant |

| ✓ | OTHER SKILLS |
|---|---|
| | I can conduct hand texturing tests of soil to determine soil type |
| | I can categorize vegetables by family type |
| | I can distinguish sweet from sour |
| | I can observe the changes in plants, fruit, and vegetables |

| ✓ | PLANNING SKILLS |
|---|---|
| | I can draw my garden plan |
| | I can choose plants to grow |

| ✓ | RE-PLANTING SKILLS |
|---|---|
| | I can plant a new vegetable garden by extracting the seeds from my vegetables |
| | I can start a seed library in my classroom with the seeds I extract from vegetables |

Teacher's comments

## Observations

## Nouns

| NATURAL ELEMENTS | PARTS OF A PLANT | OBJECTS | FRUIT & VEGETABLES | MONTHS & SEASONS | PEOPLE & ANIMALS |
|---|---|---|---|---|---|
| air | bulb | Garden in the Box | apple | January | friend |
| soil | flower | cup | banana | February | pest |
| sand | fruit | watering can | bean(s) | March | family |
| sun | leaf / leaves | bottle | carrot | April | bee |
| water | plant | thermometer | cassava | May | ladybug |
| food (nutrients) | roots | magnifying glass | eggplant | June | earthworm |
| mud | seed(s) | seed bomb | lettuce | July | snail |
| puddle | seedling(s) | window | mango | August | bug |
| dirt | stem | circle | onion | September | insect |
| ground | sprout | square | orange | October | aphid |
| sky | tree | triangle | pineapple | November | slug |
| temperature | sap | rectangle | potato | December | caterpillar |
| grass | plant cycle | oval | radish | winter | spot(s) |
| forest | | pattern | spinach | spring | stripe(s) |
| juice | | recipe | strawberry | summer | |
| | | ingredients | tomato | fall | |
| | | | zucchini | | |

## Verbs

| GARDENING | NATURE/ENVIRONMENT | ACTION | SENSES | CLASSROOM LANGUAGE |
|---|---|---|---|---|
| plant | harvest | sleep | smell | stick |
| pour | reduce | eat | taste | glue |
| sprinkle | recycle | listen | feel | trace |
| water | reuse | look | see | draw |
| fill | upcycle | touch | hear | paint |
| grow | | walk | | dip |
| squeeze | | | | print |
| compost | | | | group |
| sew | | | | measure |
| | | | | work well |
| | | | | get along |

## Adjectives

| COLORS | SIZE & SHAPE | TASTE & TEXTURE | EMOTIONS | WEATHER & TEMPERATURE |
|---|---|---|---|---|
| red | big / bigger | sweet | happy | sunny |
| orange | small / smaller | sour | sad | rainy |
| yellow | tall / taller | dry | patient | windy |
| green | long | wet | thirsty | cloudy |
| blue | round | moist | | snowy |
| purple | light | rough | | stormy |
| brown | heavy | smooth | | hot |
| black | pointy | soft | | cold |
| white | thick | furry | | warm |
| light | | bumpy | | |
| dark | | lumpy | | |
| bright | | | | |

| Adverbs | Prepositions |
|---|---|
| quietly | above |
| regularly | under |
| slowly | over |
| carefully | behind |
| indoors / inside | between |
| outdoors / outside | with |
| | near |
| | down |
| | in |

### 1. The Vegetable Plot
(Lead vocal by Aspara Gus)

In the middle of the night *(Do do do do do)*
With a shuffling sound *(Do do do do do)*
In the pale moonlight
We come out of the ground
We're part of a family
Part of a tribe
We come in all shapes and sizes and colors and types

We are The Vegetable Plot
The Vegetable Plot
The Vegetable Plot
Can you hear us grow?
It's no kind of mystery
No conspiracy
What you reap is what you sow

We are The Vegetable Plot
The Vegetable Plot
The Vegetable Plot
Can you hear us grow?
My name is Aspara Gus
And I speak for all of us
When I say we're happy you came here to see our show

Now listen
This is Sue Kini *(Hello!)*
And this is Ru Barb *(Oh, hi)*
This is Collie Flower *(Mmm Hmm)*
And this is Rockit Lettuce *(I'm Rockit Lettuce)*
They're green and leafy
And they sing so beautifully
And they're backed up by the freshest, filthiest, rootsiest band in town
BLOW!

[Sax solo]

One night under the soil
We heard music playing
We poked our heads up to try and find the source
All of a sudden
In a flash of light
We were whisked up into the air by a mysterious force

It was aliens from a place called Wambamboobaloo
In a spaceship on a transgalactic course
They fired their laser beams
And turned us into super beings
In possession of the power of the human voice
Now we're tired of being stepped on
We're gonna use music as a weapon
To electrify all the girls and boys

The Vegetable Plot *(The Vegetable Plot)*
The Vegetable Plot *(The Vegetable Plot)*
Here we come, ready or not
(x2)

[Sax solo]

The Vegetable Plot *(The Vegetable Plot)*
The Vegetable Plot *(The Vegetable Plot)*
Here we come, ready or not
(x2)

From the earth to the sky
We don´t know the reason why
Ask the guys from Wambamboobaloo
What do they do in Wambamboobaloo
I don't know, I can't say
I only met those aliens up in space
Spay-ay-ay-ace
Only met those aliens up in spay-ay-ace
Spay-ace *(Spay-ace)*
Spay-ay-ay-ace *(Spay-ace)*
Only met those aliens up in space

## 2. I Love to Go Outside
(Lead vocal by Sue Kini)

*(Sue Kini?)*
I love the morning sun
I love the bright blue sky
I love to get up early and have fun
I love to go outside

I love the smell of the sea *(Oh Sue!)*
It's a feast for my ears and my eyes *(Where are you?)*
I love to jump in and swim swim swim
I love to go outside

I love to pick up leaves that have fallen from the trees
I love to look for birds and butterflies
I love to look around and listen to the sounds
I love to go outside

When it's raining
I put on my yellow gumboots and I splash
In every muddy puddle I can find
Then it's back home I go
And drink my cocoa
I love to go outside
I love to go outside

**Did you know?** *Gumboots* are also called *wellington boots*, or *wellies*, in the UK, and *rain boots* in the USA.

## 3. The Rain Song
(Lead vocal by Collie Flower)

*Drip drop drip drop*
*Drip drop drip drop*

1
I hear footsteps on the roof
A pitter patter in the dirt
Like someone's dancing on the earth
With a thousand little feet
Each one dancing to the beat
To the beating of a drum
The rain has come
It's like the beating of a heart
A million hearts beating as one
A brand new cycle has begun
Once again the wheel has spun
The rain has come
The rain has come

[Chorus]
*And after the rain will come the sun*
*After the rain will come the sun*
*After the rain will come the sun*
*After the rain will come the sun*

2
We were born inside the soil
Reaching upward to the sky
Reaching outward to the stars
As our spaceship spun
In the ocean of the night
A tiny radius of light
Spinning circles round the sun

*The rain has come*
*The rain has come*

[Chorus]
*And after the rain will come the sun*
*After the rain will come the sun*
*After the rain will come the sun*
*After the rain will come the sun*

3
*Drip drop drip drop*
*Drip drop drip drop*

It's falling softly from above
Like whispered words of love
Upon our earth so young
The rain has come
And inside each and every drop
From the bottom to the top
The song of all of us is sung
It's where all of us begun
The rain has come
The rain has come

[Chorus]
*And after the rain will come the sun*
*After the rain will come the sun*
*After the rain will come the sun*
*After the rain will come the sun*

*Drip drop drip drop*
*Drip drop drip drop*
*Drip drop drip drop*
*Drip drop drip drop*

**4. Melon Collie**
(Lead vocal by Collie Flower)

My name is Collie Flower
I've got some friends who love me
But sometimes I still get lonely
And then they call me
Melon Collie

Sometimes I feel so happy
Like I could touch the ceiling
But sometimes how I'm feeling
Is only
Melon Collie

But when I'm feeling sad
I can write a poem
And when I'm feeling sad
I can paint a picture
When I'm feeling sad
I can sing a song
And then I won't be sad too long

We love you Collie Flower
You fill our lives with music
And music makes us jolly
Our soft and sweet
Melon Collie

When we're feeling sad
We can write a poem
And when we're feeling sad
We can paint a picture
When we're feeling sad
We sing our favorite song
And then we won't be sad too long

**5. Little Green Heads**

(Lead vocal by Aspara Gus, joined by girls in the first chorus and everyone in the second and final chorus, acapella verse)

Boys and girls (Yes?), mums and dads *(Hello!)*
Can you keep a secret?
If you can't keep a secret,
We're going to tell you anyway *(Oh!)*
And it's not really a secret
You should tell everybody you know today

You don't need to buy us in a shop *(No!)*
You don't need to buy us in the supermarket
All you need to do is take a little seed
And put it in the ground
Pour a little water on top
And then you pat it down *(pat pat pat)*

So stretch out your hand
Take a little seed and put it in the ground *(La la la la)*
Pour a little water on top and then you pat it down *(pat pat pat)*
Then wait … *(How long for?)* foooor a little while
And then you watch out… watch out *(Look out!)*
For our…

Little green heads poking up out of the dirt *(La la la la)*
Little green heads poking up out of the dirt *(La la la la)*
Little green heads poking up to say hello *(Hello!)*

[Repeat above section]

[Bridge]
Poking up to say hello *(Hello!)*
Poking up to say hello *(Hello!)*
Little green heads poking up to say hello *(Hello!)*

*Ladies and gentlestems, bulbs and girls, we were The Vegetable Plot*
*Please welcome Sue Kini, Collie Flower, Rockit Lettuce and Ru Barb.*
*In the back line, Mr Beet, Rootabaga, Purple Haze, over here Blowbergine, Tom Ato and Tine Turnip*
*And our special guests Butternunt Squash, Bro Colini and Mr Artie Choke*

*My name is Aspara Gus and we would like you to sing with all of us*

Little green heads poking up out of the dirt *(La la la la)*
Little green heads poking up out of the dirt *(La la la la)*
Little green heads poking up to say hello *(Hello!)*
(x2)

Stretch out your hand
Take a little seed, put it the ground *(La la la la)*
Pour a little water on top and then you pat it down *(pat pat pat)*
Then wait…foooor a little while
And then you watch out…
For our…

Little green heads poking up out of the dirt *(La la la la)*
Little green heads poking up out of the dirt *(La la la la)*
Little green heads poking up to say hello

**Did you know?** *Aubergine* is commonly used in the UK while in the USA it's called *eggplant*.
*Beetroot* is known simply as *beet* in the USA.

**6. Squeeze Your Vegetables/Grow Up Up Up**
(Lead vocal by Aspara Gus)

Well how do you tell
If a vegetable's ready
To go into the oven
At gas mark 20
You don't have to ask 'em
Down on your knees
You just go up and give one a little squeeze
That's right

[Chorus]
You gotta squeeze squeeze squeeze your vegetables
Squeeze squeeze squeeze your vegetables
Squeeze squeeze squeeze your vegetables
Please
Come on now

You gotta squeeze squeeze squeeze your vegetables
Squeeze squeeze squeeze your vegetables
Squeeze squeeze squeeze your vegetables
Please
What you gotta do?

You gotta hug 'em, that's how you show 'em that you love 'em
And if you really want to please 'em
All you gotta do is squeeze 'em
That's right

You gotta squeeze 'em good, squeeze 'em tight
First thing in the morning, last thing at night
Just before you give 'em a bite
You gotta sqeeze 'em

[Musical interlude] *Purple Haze!*

Well now how do you tell *(How do you tell?)*
If a vegetable's keen *(If a vegetable's keen)*
To be a part *(To be a part)*
Of today's cuisine

You don't have to tickle 'em
Or make 'em sneeze *(achooo)*
You just go up and give one a little squeeze
Come on now

[Chorus]
You gotta squeeze squeeze squeeze your vegetables
Squeeze squeeze squeeze your vegetables
Squeeze squeeze squeeze your vegetables
Please
That's right

You gotta squeeze squeeze squeeze your vegetables
Squeeze squeeze squeeze your vegetables
Squeeze squeeze squeeze your vegetables
Please
Mmm Hmm

You gotta hug 'em, that's how you show 'em that you love 'em
And if you really want to please 'em
All you gotta do is squeeze 'em
That's right

You gotta squeeze 'em good, squeeze 'em tight
First thing in the morning and last thing at night
Just before you give 'em a bite
You gotta sqeeze 'em

*Blowbergine!*
[Sax solo – transition into Grow Up Up Up]

**Did you know?** Gas mark is used in ovens in the UK to measure temperature. Typically the maximum setting would be near 10, so gas mark 20 is a great exaggeration!

## Grow Up Up Up

(Sung by Gus, everyone joins for up up up and growwww)

Grow up up up
Grow right up to the top
Up up up
And don't you ever stop
Being full of wonder at the sunshine and the thunder
Keep your dreams in sight
And grow towards the light

Grow up up up
You can grow up big or small
Up up up
Be thankful for it all
Don't forget the ones who love you and have taken good care of you
Keep them in your sight
And grow towards the light

Grow up up up
Growwwww
Up up up
Growwwww
Up is where you're going if you never stop growing
Reach to you full height
And grow towards the light

[Instrumental – kazoo and clarinet]

Grow up up up
Grow up just like a tree
Up up up
See all that you can see
Splash in water fountains and go dashing over mountains
Life is full of fun
When you grow towards the sun

Grow up up up
Be a dancer or a clown
Up up up
Or mayor of Sydney town
You could be an astronaut who flies though outer space
You could be a lawyer who also plays the bass

Grow up up up
Growwwww
Up up up
Growwwww
Up is where you're going if you never stop growing
Reach to your full height
And grow towards the light
You gotta reach to your full hei-iii-iiii-iii-iiight

And grow towards the light

## 7. Mango
(Lead vocal by Aspara Gus)

[Chorus]
*Mango mango mango*
*mango mango mango*
*mango mango mango*
*in summertime we eat mango*

1
In wintertime we eat pumpkin
in a ravioli or a dumpling
but when the summer breeze starts to blow
it's time for us all to eat mango
Mama's wearing a bikini
while Dad is smugglin' a budgie
Uncle Joe plays the charango
while the kids are eating their mango

[Chorus]
*Mango mango mango*
*mango mango mango*
*mango mango mango*
*in summertime we eat mango*

2
Cut the flesh in a criss-cross
then you arch the back till the cubes pop
that is what you call a hedgehog yo
It's the perfect way to eat mango
but if you're feeling the power
you can peel it like a flower
pop it in your teeth and dance up a tango
with your juicy juicy flower mango

[Chorus]
*Mango mango mango*
*mango mango mango*
*mango mango mango*
*in summertime we eat mango*

3
The rhythm gets into your system
breaking down your resistance
a calypso, samba or a mambo
is the dance you're doing with a mango
Uncle Zachary likes it in a daiquiri
and little Mimi likes it in an ice cream
but that's much too fancy for Django
he likes to eat the raw mango

[Chorus]
*Mango mango mango*
*mango mango mango*
*mango mango mango*
*in summertime we eat mango (x2)*

**8. Mr. Potato**
(Lead vocal by French Onion)

*Mr Potato comes from Peru*
*he's good to eat for me and you*

1
Mr Potato
has a moustache
he likes to rinse
and take hot baths
the other night
he got mashed
and the night before that
he was smashed
Mr Potato
he's versatile
with his jacket
oh he's got style

[Chorus]
*Mister Potato*
*Oh oh oh*
*Mr Potato*
*Mr Potato*

2
Mr Potato
likes company
He likes to party
with celery
Spanish onion
and mayonnaise
are his companions
on sunny days
Mr Potato
he's everywhere
in France
they call him pomme de terre
in the oven
he likes to bake
sometimes
he gets burnt by mistake

[Chorus]
*Mr Potato*
*Oh oh oh*
*Mr Potato*
*Mr Potato*

3
Mr Potato
lives in the soil
he likes to bathe
with olive oil
he loves rosemary
and tarragon
he loves dill
chilli and lemon
salt and pepper
and garlic too
he loves me
oh and he loves you
Mr Potato
so good to eat
he's the best
friend you'll ever meet

[Chorus]
*Mr Potato*
*Oh oh oh*
*Mr Potato*
*Mr Potato*
*Mr Potato*
*Mr Potato*

### 9. Sweet Corn
(Lead vocal by Ru Barb)

1
Sweet corn clinging to the cob
That's swimming in the pot
that's sitting on the hot plate
waiting for the tongs
to pick you up and drop you
on the counter top and
pop you from the top to the bottom
like
little yellow teeth with butter underneath
sometimes I feel like I was born to feast on

[Chorus]
*Sweet corn [sweet corn]*
*Sweet corn [sweet corn]*
*Sweet corn [sweet corn]*
*Come and get your eat on*

2
Sweet corn wrapped up in pale green paper
like a present waiting to be opened
and put into the water
with a crack of pepper
and a pinch of rock salt
sitting on the stovetop
then you
let it cool down for a mo or toe
then you put it to your mouth and you blow blow blow

[Chorus]
*Sweet corn [sweet corn]*
*Sweet corn [sweet corn]*
*Sweet corn [sweet corn]*
*Come and get your eat on*

Sweet corn
crunch crunch
Sweet corn
crunch crunch
Sweet corn
crunch crunch
Come and get your eat on (x2)

I don't think there's a veg been born
with a sweeter and juicier crunch than yours

[Chorus]
*Sweet corn [sweet corn]*
*Sweet corn [sweet corn]*
*Sweet corn [sweet corn]*
*Come and get your eat on*

## 10. Artie's Community Garden

(Lead vocal by Artie Choke)

*Artie*
*Artie Choke*
*He's a heartie smarty bloke*

Hello bulbs and girls, welcome to Artie's community garden
I hope you're all hungry
Cos everybody eats when they come to my patch

Hello, what's your name?
**Sean**
Sean, have some corn
and you
**Peg**
here Peg, have an egg
have a bean, Dean
have some peas, Louise
everybody eats when they come to my patch

and your name
**Jess**
have some cress
and you?
**Dale**,
here Dale, try some kale
try a leek, Zeke, eat some squash, Josh
Everybody eats when they come to my
community garden
community garden
community means you and me doing things in unity
everybody eats when they come to my patch

There's just so much food growing all over the place, can you see it?
**No**
Look closely, see

We've got Aspara Gus growing here
Rocket and Ru Barb over there
We've got Collie, Sue Kini and baby Brocolini
Everybody eats when they come to my community garden

Would you like to hear a joke?
**Yes**

Okay, what kind of vegetable do chickens grow on
**er... um**
eggplants
**[giggles]**

What about this, why did the potato go to the doctor?
Because he wasn't peeling well
**[laughs]**

Oh I've just thought of another one
Knock knock
**who's there?**
can o' peas
**canna peas who?**
can o' peas come inside the house
[Mooooo]
***that joke was rotten Artie***
ah well, we'll just put it on the compost heap
with the others now look here

We've got potato and turnip too
All that we need for a veggie stew
We've got basil, tomato, thyme and oregano
Everybody eats when they come to my

Community garden - can you sing that with me

[Chorus]
***Community garden***
*Community garden*
***Community garden***
*Community means you and me and all your friends and family*
*Everybody eats when they come to my patch*

Have you seen our chooks, look
This is Mildred - cluck
Daisy - bakerk
Margaret
Maisie
Just look at these  eggs they've been laying, aren't they amazing?

And look over here, we've got bees - this is Busby (*buzzing sound*)
Actually, I haven't got around to naming all the bees yet
The problem with bees is they tend to drone on

Oh hello, you've got your hand up, do you have a question?

**Aren't vegetables afraid of being eaten?**

Oh, what a good question. Can I tell you something? Vegetables LOVE being eaten. That's right. It's what we live for. You see, vegetables and human beings are partners. We feed you and you grow us, and the more you eat us, the healthier you'll be. You see friends, we're not scared of you, so why should you be scared of us?

Now can everyone put two fingers in the air with me and say "peas"

**PEAS**

Wonderful.

Thank you for coming along to my community garden today bulbs and girls, and remember, everybody eats when they come to my patch.

And now bulbs and girls, I'm very excited to announce that we have a live band playing at my community garden today. Please welcome, all the way from your kitchen...The Herbie Hancocks!

**11. Herbs and Spices**
(Performed by The Herbie Hancocks
Lead vocal by Star Anise and the Five Spice Girls
Band intros by Artie Choke)

[Chorus]
*Herbs and spices*
*Herbs and spices*
*Herbs and spices*
*You won't believe what they get up to when you leave them to their own devices*

1
Put on your thai basil
it's lemon thyme
to see Rosemary
For some sage advice
Cumin marjoram
it's chili outside
Lavender and Ginger
Are doing a dance called the hand chive

[Chorus]
*Herbs and spices*
*Herbs and spices*
*Herbs and spices*
*You won't believe what they get up to when you leave them to their own devices*

2
Parsley on the highway
It's just oregano day
Cinnamon in a mint condition
Chevrolet
Salt and pepper
Shake the cellar
Turn the speaker
Paprika Paprika paprika freak out!
get freakeh!

Ladies and gentlestems, introducing the members of The Herbie Hancocks

On drums Dill Collins
On bass Jalapeno Saladino
On keys Cory Ander
On guitar Turmeric Clapton
On percussion Paprika
And on vocals Star Anise and the Five Spice Girls

Outro
*Herbs and spices*
*Herbs and spices*
*Herbs and spices*
*Herbs and spices*
*Herbs and spices*
*Herbs and spices*
*Herbs and spices*
*You won't believe what they get up to when you leave them to their own devices*

## 12. Pyjamazon Jungle
(Lead vocal by Aspara Gus)

It's time to take a cruise
to the land of snooze
with your cuddly toys as your crew
hold them tight while you kiss good night
to your mum or your dad as they turn out the light
[CLICK]
the room goes dark
dark like a shark
some people are scared of the dark
but not you
not any more
cos you know that you're here to explore...

*the mystic streams of the land of dreams*
*where reality is whatever you please*
*the misty peaks where animals speak*
*and you can do anything anything anything anything*
*ANYTHING...*

[Chorus]
*In the Pyjamazon Jungle*
*jungle jungle jungle*
*In the Pyjamazon Jungle*
*jungle jungle jungle*
*Put your jim jams on jump into the Pyjamazon*
*jungle jungle jungle*

2
There's a world you know
you see it every day
A world made of stone where you dare not stray
a world of giants with feet of clay
laying down the rules that govern your play
but at night you can brush all the rules away
with a

Shuckashuckshack Shuckashuckshuckshack

Brush your teeth like a train on a train track
Shuckashuckashack shuckashuckshook
Put your pyjamas on and read a book

Maybe have a little tinkle tinkle
Maybe sing a little twinkle twinkle
Little star that's who you are
Now your bed is a flying car
Now your car is a steam-powered boat
Now your boat starts to float...

*down the mystic streams of the land of dreams*
*where reality is whatever you please*
*the misty peaks where animals speak*
*and you can do anything anything anything anything*
*ANYTHING...*

[Chorus]
*In the Pyjamazon Jungle*
*jungle jungle jungle*
*In the Pyjamazon Jungle*
*jungle jungle jungle*
*Put your jim jams on jump into the Pyjamazon*
*jungle jungle jungle*

3
Look, is that a who?
is that a lion?
is this a zoo?
are we a bird?
are we on a ship?
is this a cake?
is that a chip?
is this a tree?
is this a vine?
If we climb to the top
will we find a slide?
weeeeeeeeeeeee

*the mystic streams of the land of dreams*
*where reality is whatever you please*

*the misty peaks where animals speak*
*and you can do anything anything anything anything*
*ANYTHING…*

[Chorus]
*In the Pyjamazon Jungle*
*jungle jungle jungle*
*In the Pyjamazon Jungle*
*jungle jungle jungle*
*Put your jim jams on jump into the Pyjamazon*
*jungle jungle jungle*

**13. Under the Groun / Organic**
(Lead vocal by Aspara Gus)

Once I could be found
under the ground
Way down in the loam
that was my home
with the bugs and the worms wriggling around
under the ground
I was a tiny little seed
Till my spirit was freed
and lifted way up high into space
But I still remember my starting place

[Chorus]
*Under the ground, under the ground*
*under the ground*
*Under the ground, under the ground*
*Way down, that's where my roots can be found*

My name is Gus, I drive a green bus
filled with my friends
we meet lots of folks and play music to them
we laugh and we sing
we all jump around
all of us once lived

[Chorus]
*Under the ground, under the ground*
*under the ground*
*Under the ground, under the ground*
*Way down, that's where our roots can be found*

ORGANIC starts…

*Ladies and gentlestems, bulbs and girls*
*it's time to get up out of your flower beds*
*shake off the dirt*
*put your hands in the sky*
*do the jumping bean*
*and SING*

We're organic
A natural product of the planet
We're organic
A natural product of the planet
We're organic
we give our bodies to the soil
and the soil rewards our toil
by giving us our food
and the food makes us feel good
and good is the way we should feel

We're organic
A natural product of the planet
We're organic
A natural product of the planet
We're organic
We give our bodies to the earth
And the earth gives us our worth
by giving us our food
and the food makes us feel good
and good is the way we should feel

We're organic
A natural product of the planet
We're organic
A natural product of the planet
We're organic
We come up out of the ground
And we leave behind a sound
and the sound gets found
and the sound gets loud
and it makes us feel good

*Ladies and gentlestems, bulbs and girls*
*we have been The Vegetable Plot*
*on drums Mr Beet*
*on bass Sir Paul McCarrotney*
*on guitar Purple Haze*
*on saxophone Blowbergine*
*on percussion Paprika*
*on vocals Ru Barb, Tom Ato, Artie Choke, Blue Pumpkin, Gramma Pumpkin, Mr Potato, Red Cabbage, Bro Colini, Collie Flower*
*with special guest The Herbie Hancocks*
*and me Aspara Gus, wishing you love and peas*

Way down, that's where our roots can be found